The History of the
FRENCH FOREIGN LEGION

The History of the
FRENCH FOREIGN LEGION
from 1831 to the Present Day

DAVID JORDAN

THE LYONS PRESS

GUILFORD, CONNECTICUT

AN IMPRINT OF THE GLOBE PEQUOT PRESS

First Lyons Press edition, 2005
Copyright © 2005 Amber Books Ltd

The Lyons Press is an imprint of The Globe Pequot Press.

Editorial and Design by:

Amber Books Ltd

Bradley's Close

74-77 White Lion Street

London N1 9PF

United Kingdom

amberbooks.co.uk

Project Editor: Michael Spilling

Design: Hawes Design

10 9 8 7 6 5 4 3 2 1

ISBN 1-59228-768-9

The Library of Congress Cataloging-in-Publication Data is available on file.

Printed in Singapore

CONTENTS

History of the Legion

For the first 100 years after the unit's formation, the French Foreign Legion struggled to gain acceptance as a professional military organization. Although its political position was often uncertain, the Legion ultimately left none in doubt as to its formidable battlefield capabilities.

The French Foreign Legion owes its creation to the events of 25 July 1830, in which King Charles X was driven from the French throne. Since 1789, France had been in a state of incredible instability. The storming of the Bastille on 14 July 1789 set in motion the revolution that brought about the execution of the king and the declaration of a republic. The revolutionaries plunged Europe into war from 1793 onwards, and one of the most successful French generals, Napoleon Bonaparte, rose to high political prominence. His ascent culminated in the *Coup de Brumaire* in 1799 and Napoleon's assumption of power (reinforced in 1804 when he declared himself emperor). The Napoleonic Wars, however, culminated in his defeat and exile, and the return of the Bourbon monarchy in the form of Louis XVIII. On Louis' death in 1824, his brother Charles succeeded him.

Charles was a firm believer in the absolutism of the monarchy, hardly an attitude guaranteed to endear him to many of his subjects. His efforts to restore the clear primacy of the crown culminated in an attempt to restrict suffrage, which proved to be the spark for the July revolution. Charles fled to England (before finally settling in Prague), to be replaced by his cousin, Louis Philippe, the duke of Orleans. The choice of Louis Philippe, made by the Chamber of Deputies, was controversial. Louis Philippe was to be the head of a constitutional monarchy, and there was dispute as to his legitimacy: the 'legitimists', supporters of the Bourbons, argued that Charles X's grandson should have been made king instead.

Swiss Guards

The continuing instability was not helped by the fact that France was not alone in having a revolution. There had been uprisings in Poland, what was to become Belgium, Italy and several of the German states. With the exception of the success of those seeking an independent Belgian state, the revolutionaries had all been defeated. Many chose to head to France, where they represented a possible source of rebellion for the future. In addition, France contained a large number of foreigners amongst the ranks of its soldiers. The Bourbons, painfully aware of the fact that there were many Frenchmen who did not welcome their return, had made sure that they employed foreign mercenaries who could be relied upon to maintain royal authority. These included six regiments of Swiss Guards and the *Regiment de Hohenlohe*, the latter made up of a mixture of nationalities.

The Swiss Guards were not well liked by the French populace, and as opposition to Charles X increased during the last part of the 1820s, the Swiss Guards became embroiled in controversy. Fights broke out between the Swiss and Parisian workers in 1827 and 1828, while in October 1829, the Paris police department complained about the way in which the Swiss Guards treated local civilians.

If this was not enough, the rest of the French Army regarded the Swiss with a mixture of loathing and mistrust. To ensure their loyalty, the Swiss Guards were paid rather better than their French counterparts, with wages that were between twice and three times as high. Swiss officers held one rank above their equivalents in a French line regiment, which caused even more resentment.

These feelings culminated in a fight between the Swiss and a grenadier regiment based at

Above: King Louis Phillipe of France. His Royal Ordinance of March 1831 allowed for the establishment of a foreign legion within the French army, with the aim of bringing the large number of foreign soldiers then in France under some semblance of official control.

Versailles in November 1828. When the 1830 revolution broke out, the Swiss realized that they were in trouble. Paris was under the control of the revolutionaries before the Swiss could react, and the rank-and-file began to desert in large numbers, fearing the fate that would befall them. (There had previously been a massacre of Swiss soldiers in 1792, when they had attempted to defend Louis XVI from the mob as anger mounted over the king's supposed collusion with foreign powers in an attempt to regain his throne).

With the revolt a success, the Provisional Government set about a restructuring of its armed forces. The Guards regiments, the most privileged, influential and politicized units in the army, were disbanded, while article 13 of the new constitution proclaimed that no foreigners could serve France. The Swiss regiments were disbanded on 14 August 1830. This left the *Regiment de Hohenlohe*.

Formation

This was not the end of the story. It was clear that the disbanded soldiers might be a source of considerable unrest, and the same could be said of the large numbers of foreign revolutionaries who had flooded the country in recent years. As a result, a royal ordinance was passed on 9 March 1831, announcing the creation of a *Légion étranger* (Foreign Legion); to reinforce the point, a supplementary order was issued nine days later, making clear that Frenchmen were not allowed to join the new unit. The creation of the Legion was not before time. By early March, large numbers of foreigners had arrived at the depot which had been established at Langres with the aim of temporarily accommodating 'refugees and foreign deserters', to the extent that the depot could barely cope.

Having established a Legion, there was a further problem – who would lead it? The solution was to place Frenchmen in officer positions to bolster the small numbers of foreigners holding commissions, but this was not as easy a process as it might seem. The upheavals in France meant that a large number of officers were prematurely retired on the grounds that their loyalty was suspect. Finding replacements for them was difficult. Some new officers were found by promoting non-commissioned officers, but this was not sufficient. The government then turned to former Napoleonic officers who had been on half-pay since 1815, placed on the semi-retired list by the Bourbons (who mistrusted them). Over 1000 officers were called out of retirement by the Provisional Government, and sent to take charge of elements of the army.

The results were not propitious. Many of the newly returned officers were at an age where their military skills were long forgotten; furthermore, they discovered that the army of 1831 was rather different to the one they had left – certain drill commands had been replaced, and they frequently found themselves issuing orders that left their men bemused at the instruction given, since it no longer appeared in the drill manual.

In addition, the fact that these officers returned to their old rank created resentment amongst younger officers, who appreciated that the arrival of men with 16 or more years' seniority into their units meant that they would almost certainly not stand a chance of pro-

The *Hohenlohe* Regiment

Unlike the Swiss, the *Hohenlohe* were regarded with relative indifference by the French public. The regiment had been established under the prince of Hohenlohe-Waldenburg-Batenstein to provide a 'home' for the foreign soldiers recruited by Napoleon who wished to continue serving France after the emperor's abdication.

Unlike the Swiss, they enjoyed a fairly dull time, and by August 1830 they were garrisoned in Marseilles, where the Provisional Government forgot about them for some months. The contradiction between the constitutional position about foreigners in French service and the fact that the *Hohenlohe* were still stationed in Marseilles was not resolved.

After some confusion, the government first ordered the regiment to move to Patras, where a French force was supporting Greek efforts to gain independence from the Ottoman Empire, but before they could embark, the regiment was disbanded in January 1831. All those soldiers who wished to continue in the French Army were transferred to the 21st Light Infantry.

Right: A legionnaire aboard a camel, one of the key modes of transport in desert climes. The Legion was not slow to make use of animals to increase the endurance of patrols and the distance that they could cover. This ultimately led to the formation of mounted units and the Legion's cavalry regiment.

motion for years to come. This influx of less-than-capable officers meant that the French Army as a whole was not particularly well-off for leadership, and for the Legion, it was worse. The prospect of leading a regiment made up of foreign refugees seemed unappealing to most French officers, and it came to be regarded as a punishment to be sent to the Legion. Most officers with any ambition sought to avoid such a posting at all costs, leaving the new formation to be officered by a mix of foreigners, the incompetent and the relatively elderly (in military terms).

Unpromising Material

The first commander of the Legion, Baron Christophe Stoffel, complained bitterly that only eight out of the 26 officers sent to help him run the Legion were in any way suited to the task. Some could not speak German (the main language of the foreigners), while others were former cavalry officers trying to acquaint themselves with the rather different skills required of an infantry officer.

He went on to bemoan the fact that his administrative officer had little idea of how to administer, while another of his officers had been branded 'the worst officer in the army' in an inspection report. Stoffel was not without fault himself. He was kindly – a trait not

necessarily required when attempting to create a good regiment out of some unpromising material and lacking in experience. The inspecting general noted that one of the Legion's officers was, in fact, a woman who found the task of convincingly disguising herself as a man impossible. Stoffel was well aware of the fact that one of his officers was not male, but had not quite had the heart to dismiss her.

The general ordered Stoffel to dispense with her services, but despite reservations about Stoffel's ability as a commander, he admitted to having some sympathy – the woman was at least not actively conspiring against her commanding officer, while the two battalion commanders most definitely were.

The general noted that Stoffel's task was made more difficult by the fact that the two officers were only too eager to slander him in front of the men, although their attempts were hampered by the fact that very few of the men could understand them, since they did not speak French.

In addition to this problem, the Legion was almost totally devoid of non-commissioned officers (NCOs). An appeal to French NCOs to come out of retirement to join the Legion was met with almost total apathy, and a solution was found by appointing German university students who had fled their homeland after their activism had not brought about a successful revolution. The grounds for these appointments were less than convincing: they had a higher social position than their colleagues, and their educational background also set them apart. Unsurprisingly, the students did not necessarily prove good NCOs, not least because of the fact that the Legion included men who had been NCOs in other armies or foreign regiments, and who watched the new NCOs' attempts at leadership with a mixture of incredulity, hilarity, contempt and resentment. It remains unclear as to why those men who had formerly held non-commissioned rank were simply not returned to their previous status.

The poor organization did not stop there. The Legion found itself lacking equipment and uniforms. In theory, each man was meant to be equipped with a royal-blue tail coat, crimson trousers, a thick black cap known as a 'shako' and a heavy grey greatcoat. They should also have had a knapsack and other assorted items necessary for operating in the field, including weapons. All of these items were distinctly lacking, although the fact that weapons were in short supply was probably no bad thing, since the men were disaffected and prone to spending their time in local hostelries and causing trouble.

They were also rather disgruntled by the fact that their officers seemed less than concerned about them. The arrangements for paying the legionnaires were open to abuse, and it is not unfair to suggest that some of the officers and NCOs supplemented their pay with that of their men. The NCOs added to the difficulties, since they issued what equipment that did arrive in a haphazard fashion, often without recording to whom it had been issued or in what quantity.

The long-suffering Stoffel warned his superiors that the men were discontented, pointing to the fact that a number of them had taken to selling items of uniform or equipment to fund their drinking habits, and the lack of purpose in the Legion would lead to trouble. The legionnaires were not averse to finding trouble, and the prefect of Bar-le-Duc (the Legion's garrison town) was moved to complain that the local jail was filled with legionnaires, with over 50 per cell. His complaint was not so much that the

men had caused trouble, but the fact that the Legion seemed quite happy to leave them in jail, having forgotten about them as a result of the shoddy record keeping (and the temptation to claim that a jailed man was present on pay day so as to pocket his wages).

Stoffel was forced to call in 100 National Guards who watched over one midday roll call at which the local police arrested several men who were known to be planning a mutiny. Another 20 were arrested on suspicion of planning to desert, but charges were dropped when it was discovered that the administrative officer had failed to gain their signature for their enlistment papers. Since the men were not actually in the Legion, it was impossible for them to desert and they were released. Eventually, the government decided that it would be a very good idea if the troublesome legionnaires were not based in France.

North Africa

Conveniently, the French Army was at this point (mid 1831) fighting against pirates in North Africa. It was concluded that the best place for the Legion would be in Algiers, where the troublesome legionnaires could turn their energies towards something more useful. Stoffel's concerns about his men deserting en masse when they were marching towards Toulon (from where they would embark for Algiers) proved exaggerated. The citizens of Toulon now had to deal with the temporary presence of the Legion. Despite the problems outlined above, Stoffel and his officers had imposed some semblance of organization on the Legion, which now had six battalions. The 1st, 2nd and 3rd Battalions were made up from soldiers formerly in the Swiss Guard and the *Hohenlohe* regiments.

The 4th Battalion contained Spanish troops, the 5th Italians and Sardinians and the 6th Belgians and Dutchmen. This structure meant that the Legion was still two battalions below strength, since each French Army unit was made up of eight battalions with eight companies of 112 men. As the first elements of the Legion departed for Algiers, the 7th (Polish) Battalion was established. After it was near to strength, it was sent to join the rest of the Legion, and promptly disgraced itself when a complete platoon deserted, followed by perhaps the most spectacular piece of collective indiscipline to date, when an entire company embarked upon a drinking binge and assaulted its officers.

Despite this litany of failures, corruption and incompetence, the move to Algiers marked the first step in the Legion becoming the internationally respected unit that it is today. The fact that the Legion had something to do dealt with some of the problems that had arisen out of boredom. The 1st Battalion, appropriately enough, was the first to reach Algiers, and was put to work draining a marsh and building a road. This feat of engineering was accompanied by construction of barracks and other facilities, beginning an engineering tradition within the Legion that persists today. It was, however, nearly 12 months before the Legion was tested in battle.

Stoffel's tenure as commanding officer came to an end shortly

Above: A legionnaire in the full dress uniform worn in the period 1831–35. There is little to distinguish the legionnaire from other units in the French army, and the famed képi had not yet become part of the formation's uniform by this date.

before the battle to take Maison Carrée (see below). Stoffel's replacement, Colonel Michel Combe, arrived on 1 April, bringing with him regimental colours, an additional step in attempting to inculcate the Legion with a sense of comradeship and togetherness. Further exposure to the hardships of the desert and fighting against the Arabs also helped develop the spirit, and the Legion began to gain a reputation as a useful fighting force, a far cry from the initial disasters that had afflicted it.

Good Works

Part of the Legion's move away from being regarded as an ill-disciplined rabble came from the fact that Combe volunteered his men for more engineering duties.

The French commanding general in Algiers, the duke of Rovigo, believed that the area around Algiers should be colonized through the use of the army. One of the means to achieve this, Rovigo believed, was through a vigorous public works programme. Combe appreciated that a way of enhancing the Legion's reputation would be by gaining the approval of the commanding general, and he was not slow in volunteering his men for such tasks. These duties were not without hazard, however, since the hostile conditions faced by the legionnaires included the desert and its associated virulent illnesses. The conditions in which the legionnaires lived and worked were not conducive to good health, and it was not uncommon for large numbers of men to be hospitalized with a variety of illnesses.

Construction duties were accompanied by regular small actions, and the Legion acquitted itself well. By December 1833, when an inspection was carried out by General d'Alton, the Legion was able to give a good impression. D'Alton reported that the Legion appeared to be 'a very fine regiment'. The fighting around Algiers had, by this point, increased in intensity as the Emir of Mascara, Abd-el-Kader, led his followers in revolt against the presence of the French. Then, after a number of successes in which the Legion played its part, the action slackened again as the Emir was persuaded to negotiate. The Emir had no intention of compromise, however, and used the lull in the fighting to persuade a number of tribes to join him. By the spring of 1835, the Emir had an army 12,000 strong, and

---

First Blood at Maison Carrée

On 27 April 1832, the 1st and 3rd Battalions were given the job of taking the fortifications covering the town of Maison Carrée, a stronghold of the El Ouffia tribe. They completed the task successfully, giving the first indication that the Legion might be capable of achieving something in the service of France. The victory was slightly soured a month later when a detachment of legionnaires and cavalry was ambushed near Maison Carée. The commander of the group was Major Salomon de Musis, one of the two officers who had strenuously attempted to undermine Stoffel's authority. De Musis had made hints of cowardice against his commanding officer, and demonstrated that he had a firm grasp on the concept of cowardly behaviour in the face of the enemy by telling his subordinates that they should stand fast while he went for help.

De Musis took the 25 cavalrymen in the party with him, leaving 27 legionnaires to face the attacking tribesmen. The officer commanding the party, Lieutenant Cham, ordered his men to open fire on the attacking tribesmen, which they did. However, after the first volley Cham ordered the legionnaires to head for the cover of a small wood a short distance away.

In a European battle, this would have been a sensible idea, but in North Africa, the best means of defence was, in fact, to remain in a defensive square, volley-firing at the attackers. The legionnaires were soon surrounded, and killed or captured. Cham became the first Legion officer to die in battle, and his men all shared a similar fate. Those not killed in the battle and taken prisoner were killed when they refused to convert to Islam. One legionnaire agreed to the proposition, and was taken to the enemy camp where he was employed as slave labour. He in fact had no intention of following Islam, and escaped at the first opportunity. He made his way back to Maison Carrée, and his report was enough to damn Major de Musis. The errant officer was transferred from the Legion to a penal battalion, his reputation destroyed.

Above: Under the watchful gaze of local Arabs, legionnaires from the First Regiment take a meal by the roadside. The Legion's control of large swathes of desert was accomplished by patrols of punishing length, giving rise to one of the mottos associated with the unit: 'March or Die'.

used this to attack a column of French troops led by General Camille Trézel near Moulay Ishmael on 26 June 1835. A bitter battle ensued over the next three days, culminating with a misplaced attack on the Macta salt marshes by the Legion's 4th and 5th Battalions that ran into murderous defensive fire from the Arabs. The legionnaires were forced to retreat, and in so doing, uncovered the left flank of Trézel's column. The resulting confusion gave the Arabs the opportunity to pick off the wagon drivers, and loot the wagons at their leisure. Trézel led a cavalry charge to what was left of the convoy and having driven the enemy away, was able to withdraw. The defeat at Macta was a notable blow to the French, and the garrison at Oran was ordered to move on to the defensive instead of continuing to prosecute attacks against the enemy.

Although the Legion was criticized in some quarters for its actions at Macta (on the grounds that the attack by the two battalions was foolish and the cause of the reverse), it had far greater issues to deal with.

Departure from Africa

In 1834 Spain moved towards civil war, and the 4th Battalion, made up of Spanish legionnaires, had been disbanded as a result of a request sent to the French government from Madrid. The 7th (Polish) Battalion had renumbered as the 4th, but this could not disguise the fact that the Legion was now in danger of losing all its Spanish troops, not only in the form of those who had returned home, but also the steady stream of recruits who had previously sought to join the Legion.

In addition, the Polish and Italian battalions were showing increasing signs of fractiousness towards one another. The recently appointed commander of the Legion, Colonel Joseph Bernelle, decided that the only way to overcome this was by amalgamating all the battalions so that nationalities were mixed. This sensible step, ensuring that the Legion did not fragment into national factions, was enacted on 17 August 1835 – the very day that the French government handed control of the Legion over to Spain.

The Spanish Carlist wars began with the death of King Ferdinand VII

of Spain. His successor was the three-year-old Queen Isabella II. Her mother, Queen Maria Christina, assumed the role of regent, but the late king's brother, Don Carlos, disputed the succession, claiming that the throne was his. Don Carlos based his claim on the fact that Ferdinand had altered the laws of succession.

Traditionally, the Spanish monarchy had allowed either male or female heirs, but Salic law, in which women were excluded from the line of succession, had been introduced in the eighteenth century. Don Carlos and his supporters claimed that Ferdinand's decision to revert to the traditional law of succession was invalid, and moved to take the throne.

Although the French were sympathetic to Isabella, there was considerable reluctance to become involved. Louis-Phillippe feared that intervention in Spain might shake his position on the throne, and many senior figures, painfully aware that the Peninsular War had been a painful experience for France, advised caution.

However, the decision of the British and Portuguese governments to send aid to Isabella prompted the minister of the interior, Adolphe Thiers, to persuade his cabinet colleagues that France could not afford to remain aloof from the conflict. If it did, he argued, French influence in Spain would be eroded.

Right: Sergeant-Major Doze grabs the enemy colours as the battle of Constantine draws to a close on 13 October 1837. The battle was one of a series fought in Africa as the French took control of Algeria.

Left: A legionnaire takes a brief rest, somewhere in Spain in 1837. The 'Old' Legion came to an end in the Spanish campaign: handed over to the Spanish monarchy, it was poorly employed and suffered from neglect by its new employers. The troops were left in ragged uniforms until an outcry in France led to supplies of more clothing being sent; shortly after this, the Spanish dispensed with the Legion's services and returned it to French control.

Spanish Adventure

As a compromise, it was decided that the Legion offered the best solution – foreign troops in the pay of France, rather than Frenchmen, would provide the means for maintaining French influence in Spain. Placing them under Spanish control meant that if the commitment became difficult, France would not be faced with the problem of trying to extricate its forces from Spain. Madrid would control the Legion's activities, neatly allowing the French Government to show its commitment to Isabella's cause, but without any of the problems associated with extricating forces from a difficult commitment.

The decision to hand the Legion over to Spanish control did not go down well with the legionnaires. Although many would have been quite content to go to Spain as representatives of their adopted country, there were very few who were pleased to find that they were now part of the Spanish Army instead. Officers who were unhappy with the prospect were allowed to transfer to other regiments, or, if they had joined the Legion straight from civilian life, to return to their homes. In a bid to

Above: A stylised portrait showing the legion in action against Abd-el-Kader's cavalry at some time in 1840. Abd-el-Kader was a formidable opponent, and it took the Legion until 1857 to bring Algeria finally under full French control.

prevent a mass departure by officers, the government offered promotions to those officers who agreed to go (only to refuse to recognize the promotions when the officers eventually returned to French service). This was not enough to prevent the departure of a number of the French officers, and several of the foreign officers left the Legion in disgust, arguing that they wished to serve France, not Spain.

While the officers had a choice, the legionnaires did not. They found that Colonel Bernelle intended to make a number of changes to the organization that went further than his original step of making the battalions multi-national. The multi-national battalions still contained companies made up almost entirely of one nationality; Bernelle changed this, mixing the personnel of each company without regard for nationality, and making French the common language. While this move caused initial difficulties, it did much to ensure that the various elements of the Legion could actually understand one another,

making for a far more efficient fighting force, as coordination of the troops became a far simpler task. Bernelle, a veteran of the Peninsular War and deeply distrustful of the Spanish, decided that he would not rely upon his new employers, and set about creating an all-arms force made up of infantry, engineers, artillery and cavalry, a move that helped to establish the tradition of versatility within the Legion.

These improvements were not enough to disguise the fact that the Legion had, to all intents and

Above: Legionnaires storm a Carlist position in Spain during the fierce and bloody fighting of 1836. The Legion's reputation as an elite force began to develop during this campaign, despite the privations suffered by the soldiers during the Legion's time under Spanish control.

purposes, been abandoned by the French Government. The legionnaires noticed that the arrival of their pay became erratic, and that the war they were being asked to fight was particularly brutal – there were atrocities on both sides, and the customs of war were not always followed. There are strong suspicions that the Legion's reorganization was financed by taking a dozen wealthy Spaniards hostage and using the ransom to buy the necessary equipment to establish the artillery and cavalry units under Bernelle's reforms.

The war continued throughout 1836, and the Legion began to gather a reputation as fierce fighters, willing to fight to the finish. The apparent enthusiasm to fight for a lost cause made the Carlists rather more prudent when tackling the Legion, and in one month (April)

the legionnaires killed over 1000 Carlists, while taking 300 fatal casualties themselves.

Despite the growing success of the Legion, Bernelle was increasingly concerned about the growing levels of desertion as his men, unwilling servants of Spain in the first place, voted with their feet as the Spanish Government proved unable to pay them on time. Bernelle made an appeal to both the French and Spanish governments on his troops' behalf, and was sacked for his trouble, despite all the good he had done. His replacement was utterly incompetent and sacked after a month, and he in turn was replaced by Colonel Joseph Conrad, who had served with the Legion since its earliest days in Algiers.

Conrad was a wealthy man, and dealt with the problem of pay by the simple expedient of providing wages from his own pocket. He could not, however, solve the problem of the lack of clothing. By the end of 1836, the legionnaires were clothed in rags, and the French press was filled with stories of the disgraceful condition of French troops (neatly ignoring the fact that the Legion was now officially Spanish). The embarrassment forced the French Government to send supplies, but it was not long before the Legion ceased to be a problem for the government.

After a bloody fight at Huesca on 24 May 1837, in which 20 officers and 350 men died, the Legion was reduced to a single battalion, and worse was to follow. On 2 June, Conrad led his men into battle at Barbastro. He was one of the first to fall, killed by a shot to the head. The

legionnaires fought on, and by the end of the day only 130 men were left alive. They had inflicted heavy casualties on the enemy, claiming over 700 of their opponents, but this bloody fight was to be their last. The battalion stayed on in Spain, camped near Saragossa until the Spanish Government brusquely told them that it had no further use for them.

They marched back to France and arrived to find that the old Legion was dead, and a new one had arisen in its place. All the survivors volunteered for service with the new Legion, and were rewarded with a loss of seniority and a refusal to recognize any promotions or gallantry awards gained in Spain. It was as though the French Government and the army wished to forget all about the waste of the Legion in Spain.

Rebirth

While the 'old' Legion was in Spain, it became clear to the French Government that they had, perhaps, made a mistake in handing the force over. The demands for manpower in Algeria had not declined, and there were still large numbers of foreigners in France, who, the government felt, would be less dangerous in the ranks of the Legion.

As a result, Louis-Phillipe signed an Ordinance on 16 December 1835 in which authority was given for the creation of a 'new' Legion. This date marks the founding of the Foreign Legion that exists today, but the 'old' Legion's work should not be ignored, since much of what was done influenced the way in which the 'new' Legion went about its work.

The new formation was sent to Algiers, and this was to be the Legion's home for another century. Fighting continued until 1882, when it was announced that Algeria had been 'pacified'. Algeria was slowly drawn under French control as generals expanded the area of territory under French ownership, although resistance was fierce. The Legion ground down the opposition, and Abd-el-Kader's forces were driven into the desert and a nomadic lifestyle, their villages destroyed in the fighting. In 1844, the Legion dealt a further serious blow to Arab resistance when Abd-el-Kader himself was defeated when the Legion stormed his camp. The attack was led by the duke of Aumale, and the success of his assault (the Legion lost nine men to at least 300 Arab casualties) made him a national hero.

Abd-el-Kader was forced to retreat to Morocco, but his plans to harass French shipping were curtailed when the Moroccan Army was defeated by a French force at Isly in August 1844. Abd-el-Kader surrendered in 1847 and was imprisoned before being exiled to Damascus. Ironically, this bitter enemy of France ended his days as a much-liked celebrity, complete with the award of the *Légion d'honneur*. The latter was gained when he intervened to save over 12,000 Christians from the Turks. His new-found respectability in French society enabled him to set up a huge library in his home, and he travelled extensively around Europe. Perhaps the final mark of his rehabilitation was his invitation to the opening of the Suez Canal, the most obvious sign of colonization in North Africa.

While Adb-el-Kader enjoyed his retirement, the French set about colonizing Algeria with considerable vigour. By the 1880s, over a million Europeans were living in Algeria, defended in part by the Legion that had done so much to establish the French position in the country. Although Algeria had become the Legion's spiritual home by the latter years of the nineteenth century, it had fought in a number of other places, increasing its reputation in the process.

War upon War

While the Legion was establishing its permanent home in Algeria, many of its constituent elements were to fight across the globe in the

Above: Colonel Combe, commander of the Legion in 1832. Combe was the second commander of the Legion, and did much to deal with the disciplinary problems that the unit faced. He handed over command after only a few months, but was to meet his death alongside men he had once led, killed in the assault on Constantine in 1837.

Above: Legionnaires advance towards Ischeriden on 24 June 1857. The battle marked the point at which Kabyle resistance in Algeria came to an end, enabling the French to claim that pacification of the area was complete.

pursuit of French interests. The first location for conflict was, in fact, Paris itself. In 1848, Louis-Phillipe was overthrown after his scheme to reduce unemployment in Paris met with popular outrage – the unemployed wanted jobs, but the king's proposed solution of employing them in the army was not to their liking. Riots broke out and although suppressed by the National Guard, the king fled.

His successor was Louis Bonaparte (Napoleon's nephew), elected president, the head of the Second Republic. Louis, like his uncle, was not particularly impressed by the idea that he might be replaced after an election. He staged a coup of his own in 1851, declaring himself Emperor Napoleon III and sowing the seeds for later confusion as historians wondered what had happened to Napoleon II. (Napoleon II was the first Napoleon's son, but who had, of course, never ruled France – a fact that did not prevent Bonapartists, if no-one else, from referring to him as Napoleon II.)

Although Napoleon III declared that the new empire was going to be peaceful, he continued the policy of increasing French influence and territories around the world. The first display of this came in 1854, when France and Britain declared war on Russia after the latter's efforts to control Istanbul, and sent forces to the Crimean peninsula.

Italian Adventure

Following the end of the Crimean War, the French Government disbanded the 1st Foreign Legion and sent them back to the Algerian base at Sidi-bel-Abbès, where they

Above: Legionnaires taking the town of Zaatcha on 26 November 1849. This was the second assault of the year on the Saharan oasis held by the Chaouia tribe, and the first had been driven off. The second attack took six weeks to complete, and the tribesmen were driven out at the point of the bayonet. Over 1500 legionnaires had been killed or wounded by the end of the battle.

joined the 2nd Regiment in the continued pacification of the new French territory. A new 1st Regiment was established, filled with fresh recruits from Switzerland, undermining the principle of mixed companies and battalions at a stroke.

Although the Crimean veterans had been sent to Algeria, they soon returned to Europe when Napoleon III decided that he wished to support the unification of the Italian states. His stance inevitably meant conflict with Austria, which controlled a number of the states and did not wish to see its influence or territory diminished by Italian unification. Napoleon III's support for

the nationalists stemmed from the prospect of acquiring Nice and Savoy, but the risks posed by war were substantial.

The Austrians could, in the end, rely upon support from Prussia, and if the war dragged on it seemed quite probable that the Prussians would intervene. Meetings with the Italian nationalist prime minister of Piedmont, Camillo di Cavour, took place in July 1858, and it was agreed that the French would intervene the following year. Cavour provoked the Austrians into declaring war in April 1859, and the French immediately offered assistance. Napoleon decided to lead his army person-

ally, and set off at the head of a 140,000 strong force. The Legion was part of this expeditionary force, with the 1st and 2nd Regiments banded together for the campaign as the 1st Regiment was well below strength. The French and Austrian armies met outside Magenta on 4 June 1859.

Napoleon III appears to have been under the misapprehension that Magenta was lightly held, if at all, and his decision to send forces to occupy the town may have been different had he appreciated how well the terrain leant itself to the defence. The initial French advance went well, but it was not long before the Austrians were spotted.

The Crimean War

The Crimean War (1853–56) was marked by bloody fighting, outbreaks of disease (particularly cholera) and incompetence all round. The Anglo-French alliance was not helped by the fact that the commander of the British force, Lord Raglan, could never quite master the notion that the Napoleonic wars were over, and continued to refer to the opposition as 'the French' for the duration of the war.

The Legion found itself wintering in trenches outside Sebastopol, attempting to endure the appalling weather. The siege dragged on into 1856, and pressure from Napoleon III led to the first attack on 1 May. The French seized a Russian outpost, losing the commanding officer of 1st Foreign Legion in the course of the attack along with 117 of his men.

Further assaults on the port proved fruitless until September, when an artillery bombardment lasting three days provided sufficient cover for allied forces to approach the city walls and take the fortress by storm.

The British, French and Turkish armies then moved on to the last centre of Russian resistance at Kinburn. Unlike Sebastopol, this fell after a five-hour battle, effectively bringing the war to a close.

Above: A legionnaire contemplates conditions in the Crimea. The makeshift winter clothing and generally tatty disposition of the legionnaire highlight the harsh conditions under which much of the fighting in the Crimea was carried out. The number of deaths from disease and hypothermia rivalled battle casualties as the main cause of fatalities in the campaign.

Left: Colonel de Chabrière is killed as he leads the charge at the Battle of Magenta on 4 June 1859. De Chabrière led the legion forward as the attack against the Austrian positions began to falter; despite his death, the momentum of the assault he had launched was enough to drive the Austrians out and bring victory.

The 1st Legion Regiment went in to the attack, but was outnumbered. The Austrians fell back, but upon realizing the size of the force ranged against them, steadied themselves. At this point, the 2nd Regiment's commanding officer, Colonel Louis de Chabrière, ordered his men to charge, and the Austrians resumed their retreat in the face of this attack.

De Chabrière, however, did not live to see the success, being shot from his saddle moments after the charge began. The Legion, supported by *zouave* regiments (infantry regiments first raised in Algeria in 1831), drove the Austrians through the town. It appeared that the French attack had succeeded, and reports reached the French high command that Magenta had fallen. This proved to be optimistic.

Although some of their troops had left Magenta, the Austrians were still present in strength. The troops at their disposal included elite Tyrolean mountain troops and Croatians. The latter had a fearsome reputation, and were renowned for their willingness to resort to brutality. Douglas Porch, the author of the most authoritative history of the Legion, has noted that the Croatians' behaviour was such that they 'single-handedly might have inspired the Geneva Convention of 1864'.

After a brief pause to bring the Imperial Guard into the line, the French attack resumed. The Legion was at the forefront of the fighting, and ran straight into heavy Austrian defences. The Austrians inflicted heavy losses, and two attacks by the legionnaires failed. The third, led by Lieutenant Colonel Jose Martinez – a Spanish Carlist officer who had been so impressed by his opponents that he had left Spain to join the Legion – succeeded in breaking in to the town, but it took until dawn the following day before Magenta was firmly in French hands. The immediate aftermath of the battle was marked by farce – surviving French troops 'liberated' large quantities of wine and promptly rendered themselves incapable of further fighting for the next day or so. On 7 June, sobriety largely restored, the French marched into Milan, welcomed as liberators. Despite the success, Napoleon III began to have doubts about the wisdom of prosecuting his campaign much further. He moved on in pursuit of the Austrians, who retreated to the east. They halted and prepared to dig in, but the pursuing French forces came into contact with the Austrians just after dawn on 24 July, near to Solferino. A series of confused and bloody contacts took place, and it soon became clear to both sides that they were in the midst of another major battle.

By the middle of the afternoon, the French had suffered heavy losses. The Legion had been in the thick of the fighting, occupying the village of Cavriana, only to be driven out by a counter-attack. Austrian cavalry broke through in the centre, but a failure to follow up this success meant that the French position was not as grave as it might have been. By this point, Napoleon III was deeply concerned, and ordered a final assault. The Legion charged back into Cavriana, and its momentum was such that resistance crumbled. To the Legion's flank, Algerian troops seized the heights of Fontana, routing the opposition. The attack by the Legion and the Algerians presented an opportunity for cavalry to get behind the Austrians. Despite heavy losses amongst the French cavalry regiments, they had gained the upper hand. Under attack from the rear as well as to their front, the Austrians broke and retreated in the middle of a torrential rain storm.

His doubts about remaining in Italy increasing, Napoleon III set about negotiating a peace settlement with the Austrians. He had begun to appreciate that a united Italy might pose a threat to French power in the region. News that the Prussians appeared to be mobilizing convinced him that the time was propitious to end his Italian adventure, which could be presented as a convincing success, even if a total victory for Piedmont had not been achieved.

The French returned home, and the Legion was allowed to participate in the victory parade through Paris in recognition of its part in the campaign. This was the first time

Napoleon III

Charles Louis Napoleon Bonaparte (20 April 1808 – 9 January 1873) was the nephew of Emperor Napoleon I of France. He fought in Italy alongside nationalists campaigning for independence before becoming involved in French domestic politics. He was imprisoned after a coup attempt in August 1840, but escaped to Britain six years later. He returned to France in 1848 after the revolution, and was elected President on 2 December of that year. Harbouring a desire to recreate the empire of his uncle, he overthrew the republic exactly three years after his election, and proclaimed himself Emperor Napoleon III (Napoleon II, the title used by Napoleon I's son, was not legitimate, since he never sat on the French throne).

Napoleon III was responsible for rebuilding much of Paris, and helped develop French industry. The French economy grew during his reign, becoming the second largest in the world. These positive developments are often forgotten when assessing Napoleon III because of the disastrous results of his attempts to increase French prestige and deal with the challenge presented by the German states. While the Crimean War and intervention in Italy were successful, the German states grew in influence, particularly after 1866 with the Prussian victory over Austria. Unable to bring himself to ally with the Austrians, Napoleon III stumbled into war with Prussia in 1870. The result was a disaster: Napoleon was captured at the Battle of Sedan on 2 September 1870, and overthrown two days later. He fled to Britain, where he died in 1873.

that the Legion had been feted in public – but the legionnaires were not given time to revel in this honour, since they were immediately confined to barracks after the parade and told to make themselves ready to head back to Algiers. This treatment demonstrated once again the rather ambivalent attitude the French Government had towards the Legion. On the one hand, there was no doubt that the unit had garnered an enhanced reputation as proficient soldiers, with increasing numbers of battle honours through the 1850s. As well as success in Algeria, the Legion had acquitted itself well in the Crimea and now in Italy. On the other hand, though, it appears that a Legion made up of foreigners was regarded with a hint of suspicion and perhaps even embarrassment, hence the desire to ensure that it spent as little time as necessary in France.

It would take some years yet before the Legion was to be regarded with pride despite its non-French character, but such acceptance was, perhaps, bound to come as it added to its martial reputation. The Legion's next adventure, in Mexico, simply added to the legend.

Mexico

Between 1857 and 1860, Mexico was in a state of civil war, and as a consequence of this costly conflict, the president, Miguel Miramon, covered some of the nation's debts by issuing bonds to European investors. The bonds proved worthless, and the damage this did to the Mexican economy was such that Miramon's successor, Benito Pablo Juarez, suspended payment of

Above: Two legionnaires demonstrate the uniform worn in Mexico. While the red trousers and dark blue jacket are almost identical to the 1831 uniform, the man on the left wears the white képi cover that was to become synonymous with the Legion. His colleague wears a broad-brimmed sun hat, an item of clothing that remained popular with legionnaires in warmer climes until the latter part of the nineteenth century.

foreign debts. The investors – who even without the benefit of hindsight could be said to have been rather foolhardy – were incensed, and demanded that their governments take military action.

The British, Spanish and French governments were persuaded by the case, and decided that a joint

effort was necessary. On 31 October 1861, they signed a convention in which they agreed to occupy the Mexican fortresses at Vera Cruz, Cordoba, Tehuacan and Orizaba as a means by which they could impose their will on the Mexicans and recover their investment. Juarez reluctantly accepted

Left: Captain Danjou encourages his men as they hold out against Mexican attack at Camerone. Danjou's efforts to maintain his men's morale against impossible odds led to his death when he was shot by a Mexican sniper as he moved around the Legion's positions. The story of his sacrifice made Danjou one of the Legion's most revered historical figures.

this intervention, since the allied powers at least suggested that their presence would be temporary (until the money had been recovered) and that attempting to colonize Mexican territory was not their intention. Napoleon III, however, appears to have regarded this promise as being nothing more than an inconvenience, since he wished to impose a new Francophile monarch on Mexico, giving France a valuable foothold on the American continent. His choice fell upon Maximilian of Austria, brother of the emperor Franz Josef, and in a demonstration of the workings of diplomacy, the two nations that had been engaged in bitter fighting just three years before began negotiations to install the eager would-be monarch on the Mexican throne.

In December 1861 the European force, comprising 7000 Spaniards, 2500 Frenchmen and 700 Royal Marines (perhaps demonstrating that the British Government was not as committed to the expedition as its allies) landed and occupied Vera Cruz. The occupation was not a success, and the troops were beset with disease, as well as facing attacks from local inhabitants. The British and Spanish forces withdrew in April 1862, but Napoleon was now free to try to put his plan for Mexico into action.

Since the United States was fighting a civil war, he could be confident that there would be little, if any, American interference with his plans.

However, the Mexicans had other ideas, and when the French marched on Mexico City, they were driven back at Puebla on 5 May. Undaunted, Napoleon III sent reinforcements – and discovered that the guerrilla war that the French presence had unleashed demanded an ever-increasing supply of manpower. It was not surprising, therefore, when the Legion was chosen to be sent to bolster the forces in Mexico.

Napoleon III toyed with the idea of handing over the Legion to Maximilian, with the intention that it would remain under French control until Maximilian was securely upon the throne, whereupon it would be placed under the authority of the Mexican government. The first part of this process, of course, was to send the Legion to Mexico, and it was duly despatched on 9 February 1863. Two battalions and associated support elements left Mers-el-Kébir, arriving at Vera Cruz on 28 March. They arrived at a bad moment. The French campaign had reached something of a stalemate, with the Mexicans holding off the attackers at Puebla. To its disappointment, the Legion was not sent to join the French forces there, but given the apparently boring task of escorting supply convoys and carrying out guard duties.

The rationale for this lay in the attitude of the French commander, General Forey, who made clear that the Legion was guarding an area in which disease was rife – he preferred that foreigners, rather than

Frenchmen, should face the rigors of confronting these conditions.

The Legion soon found that there was rather more to contend with than just disease, however. Mexican guerrillas began attacking convoys, giving the legionnaires their first taste of action when a guerrilla force attacked a railway work camp. It appears that the guerrillas were expecting a relatively easy time, but the small squad of legionnaires slaughtered the attackers.

Heroes of Camerone

General Forey was well aware that he needed to break the siege at Puebla. He also appreciated the need to pay his men. As a result of these requirements, he arranged for a convoy of guns, ammunition, food and the outstanding wages to be sent from Vera Cruz to Puebla, a journey of some 241km (150 miles). Given the appalling condition of Mexican roads, it was clear that the convoy would take some time to arrive. It was arranged that the Legion would escort the convoy from La Soledad to Chiquihuite, where another unit would take control. On 27 April, Colonel Pierre Jeanningros sent two under-strength companies to meet the approaching convoy. Two days later, he was approached by a local informant, who told him that the convoy was going to be attacked by a Mexican regular formation under Colonel Mariano Camacho Milan and Colonel Angel Lucido Cambas. Cambas had benefited from a military education in France, which suggested that he could be a difficult opponent, not least since he appreciated the way in which French forces operated.

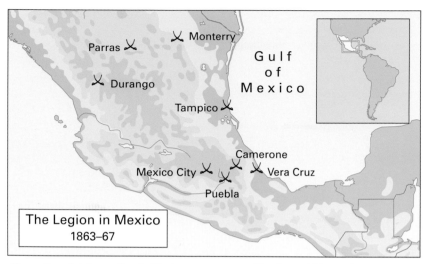

Parras
Monterry
Durango
Tampico
Gulf
of
Mexico
Camerone
Mexico City
Vera Cruz
Puebla

The Legion in Mexico
1863–67

Above: French intervention in Mexico was prompted by the ambitions of Napoleon III, but the Mexicans proved to be far more robust opponents than the French emperor had imagined. The Legion fought a number of intense engagements against Mexican troops, including the famed last stand at Camerone.

Jeanningros decided to send another company on patrol with the intention of making contact with the convoy at Palo Verde. He chose 3rd Company of the 1st Battalion. Unfortunately, all of the company's officers were ill, so Jeanningros gave command to Captain Jean Danjou. Danjou was a well-regarded Legion veteran. He had won the *Légion d'Honneur* medal in Crimea, and had seen active service in Algeria and Italy. Danjou had remained in the Legion despite a serious accident – he had lost a hand in an explosion. He had been determined not to let this injury hinder his career, and had replaced his missing hand with an impressive artificial one (it was carved and articulated, complete with flexible joints, and attached to his wrist by a leather cuff). Danjou had mastered the new hand with surprising ease, and was said to be as proficient a horseman with one hand as some were with two. Two

NCOs were promoted to the rank of *sous-lieutenant* and joined the patrol, which was little more than half strength. The patrol left the Legion headquarters in the early hours of 30 April.

The company made one stop along their route at a Legion outpost for food and coffee before pressing onwards. Shortly after first light, they passed several settlements, including Camerone, which was little more than a collection of a few farmhouses. The company soon reached Palo Verde, where it stopped for breakfast. Danjou posted sentries, and the men waited for the arrival of the convoy. However, before breakfast could be taken, the sentries signalled that a dust cloud was approaching from the west.

The legionnaires were impressed that they would not have to wait long for the arrival of the convoy, since the prospect of remaining in Palo Verde for any length of time

was not appealing. Danjou, however, was puzzled. The dust cloud was approaching from the west. It took very little time for him to appreciate that this could mean only one thing – the approaching cavalry were not part of the French convoy, but were Mexicans.

Danjou realized that the flat, barren terrain around Palo Verde was hardly the place to meet a cavalry charge, so he ordered his men to head back to Camerone. The legionnaires quickly broke camp and headed off to their new defensive position. As the company neared Camerone, a single shot rang out and struck legionnaire Pierre Conrad in the leg. Danjou sent a party of legionnaires towards the settlement, only to find the sniper had vanished. The sound of the shot, however, travelled and was enough to alert the Mexican cavalry to the presence of the French column.

The Mexicans promptly prepared to attack. The legionnaires formed a defensive square and watched as the Mexican cavalry approached at a walk. When they were about 60m (196ft) away from the French position, they began their charge. Danjou let them gain 10m (32ft), and then gave the order to fire.

The legionnaires put down sufficient weight of fire to inflict casualties on the enemy, and the Mexicans broke off the attack to reorganize. While they were doing this, Danjou moved his men so that they were now on a small rise. The Mexicans attacked again, and were driven off. However, despite the fact that two charges had been driven away, Danjou was under no illusions about the situation: in the open, the legionnaires would inevitably suffer more and more casualties until the Mexicans were able to break through. While the Mexicans regrouped following their second charge, Danjou ordered his men into a farm, the Hacienda de la Trinidad.

The position was far from ideal. Although the farm offered some protection, it was not meant to be used as a fortified position. The walls to the farmyard had several entrances that needed rapid attention to shore up, and visibility from the farmyard was negligible. Although the Mexicans could not see what Danjou was doing, he was equally unable to see the Mexicans. One of the NCOs, Sergeant Morzycki, was helped onto the roof and climbed to its highest point. His report was not encouraging. Hundreds of Mexicans were surrounding the legionnaires, and it appeared that they were willing to wait. They knew that the legionnaires would soon run out of water, and that only the timely arrival of a relief column could save them.

The Mexicans took to sniping at the legionnaires, an activity interspersed with occasional attempts at breaking through the weak spots in the wall. While Danjou and his men were able to fend off these assaults, their position was no better. At about 9:30, a Mexican officer approached under a white flag.

He offered Danjou the option of an honourable surrender, and guaranteed that the legionnaires would be treated properly as prisoners of war. Danjou was unimpressed. The Mexicans did not appear to have any heavy weapons, nor did there seem to be any infantry with them.

Danjou concluded that the threat

Captain Jean Danjou

Jean Danjou is possibly the most famous Legion officer in history, for it was his fate to be in command at Camerone in 1863. Danjou served with the Legion in Italy, Algeria and the Crimea, gaining decorations for gallantry and a reputation as a calm, competent officer who remained unperturbed whatever the situation. This composure was demonstrated in the aftermath of the accident with a faulty artillery piece that cost him his left hand. Once he had recovered, Danjou arranged for a rather complicated wooden hand to be constructed. This had fully articulated joints, and attached to his arm with a leather cuff. Danjou adapted himself to the artificial hand, and could control his horse as well as anyone else.

At Camerone, his bravery was to cost him his life – calmly walking about the Legion's defensive positions, encouraging his men, he was shot by a Mexican sniper. After the epic battle ended, his hand was found by a local rancher, who sold it back to the Legion in 1865. The hand was placed in a glass case, and is now one of the most important items in the Legion's museum, treated with reverence and paraded each year on Camerone Day. Danjou's hand is the nearest thing that the Legion has to a religious relic.

to his position was relatively slight, and politely declined the offer. As the Mexican officer returned to his position, Danjou made each of his legionnaires swear that they would fight to the death. There was no opposition to this, not least since his men were confident that they would be able to hold off cavalry until relief arrived.

They were generally of the view that the Mexicans were not particularly valiant soldiers, and felt that the enemy would melt away as soon as a relief force appeared. It was not to be.

Last Stand

The situation deteriorated from this point onwards. The Mexican cavalry were, in fact, the leading element of a much larger force, and the infantry were not far behind them. In addition, local inhabitants came to join the besieging force and added to the volume of fire directed against the legionnaires. As their infantry came up, the Mexican cavalry continued to fire upon the legionnaires and carry out sallies against the walls of the farmyard. Danjou was coordinating the defences on both sides of the yard, and took one risk too many. Just before mid-day, he presented a perfect target to a Mexican sniper, and was killed by a single shot to the chest.

It was not long before the Mexican infantry arrived. Once again, surrender terms were

Left: The end of the battle at Camerone as Mexican troops move in on the few legionnaires left standing. The bravery and persistence of the legionnaires amazed their captors, who treated their prisoners with considerable respect.

Above: Captain Danjou's wooden hand – sometimes referred to as the Foreign Legion's 'holy relic' – which is brought out and paraded on every Camerone Day, the major ceremony in the Legion's year.

offered, and the legionnaires, loyal to the vow they had made to Danjou, refused. The battle resumed, and the Mexicans gained the upper hand. They set light to bales of straw piled against the north wall of the farmyard, and one of the buildings on that side caught fire. The smoke was thick and choking, and the legionnaires responded by firing at anything that moved towards them through the smoke. The smoke began to asphyxiate and blind the men, and the heat of the flames added to the terrible thirst that tortured them. French casualties increased as the afternoon wore on, but the Mexicans were astonished at the ferocity of the resistance they faced; they were also taking heavy casualties as assault after assault was met with heavy French fire.

As the afternoon drew to a close, the Mexicans had suffered fatalities in the hundreds. However, there were very few legionnaires left alive. By 17:00, there were just a dozen legionnaires left in any condition to fight, and the Mexicans made yet another offer of an honourable surrender. Again, this was refused.

The Mexicans put in another assault, and by the end of this, only five men were left standing from 3rd Company, but they were still fighting. However, they were now down to their last round. Sous-Lieutenant (Second Lieutenant) Clément Maudet decided that their last gesture would be to charge the Mexicans, and he led the survivors out, bayonets fixed. As the astonished Mexicans opened fire, legionnaire Catteau threw himself in front of Maudet and was hit 19 times, saving his officer from certain death (although Maudet was still wounded). The Mexicans

then stopped firing to see what the three men left on their feet – Louis Main, a Prussian named Wenzel and legionnaire Constantin – would do next.

Honourable Surrender

Surrounded, the legionnaires prepared to charge the Mexicans, but before anything could happen, Colonel Cambas stepped forward, between his own men and the legionnaires. His ability to speak French now came in useful. Cambas looked at the legionnaires and said simply: 'Surrender.' Corporal Main, despite the unfavourable odds, attached conditions – they would surrender only if they could keep their weapons and treat the wounded Lieutenant Maudet. Cambas told Main that he agreed, and the legionnaires finally gave up. Cambas offered one arm to Main, and the other to the wounded legionnaire Wenzel, while his men brought up a stretcher to carry the wounded Maudet. The Mexicans treated the legionnaires more like guests than prisoners, and took them to meet Milan. Cambas introduced them, and the astonished Milan produced one of the first famous quotes about legionnaires: 'Truly, these are not men, but devils!'

The Mexicans kept their part of the surrender terms. They searched the farm buildings and discovered that there were other legionnaires left alive, all wounded. They found 23, but missed Danjou's drummer, Lai, who had hidden under a pile of corpses. He waited for the Mexicans to leave before dragging himself along the road towards the Legion headquarters at Chiquihuite. It is likely that Lai would have died on the way, but he was found by Colonel Jeanningros, who had been told of the battle by local informants on 30 April. Jeanningros set out the next day with a small party of men, and they found Lai as they neared Camerone.

When they reached the site of the battle, Colonel Jeanningros discovered that the Mexicans had removed all the bodies from the engagement, and had placed them in a nearby ditch. Concerned that the Mexicans might still be in the area, Jeanningros took the prudent decision to head back to base and assemble a larger force before returning.

This larger force finally met with the convoy on 3 May and safely escorted it to the point at which the Legion handed over responsibility for the escort to other troops. Colonel Jeanningros made sure that the bodies of the dead legion-naires were buried with full military honours.

Aftermath

The prisoners taken at the battle were later exchanged for a similar number of Mexican captives, and this allowed the Legion to ascertain the true casualty figures. The Legion 3rd Company had lost three officers and 29 men. Four of the dead had been amongst the survivors taken prisoner, but they had

Above: A group of legionnaires wearing their dress uniforms pose for the camera towards the end of the nineteenth century. The képi has replaced previous headgear, although it is still the same colour as those worn by other army units: wearing the white képi cover as a sign to distinguish the Legion did not gain official approval until the twentieth century.

died of their wounds in Mexican captivity. Four other legionnaires had simply disappeared, and their fate remains unknown. The battle at Camerone had been sufficient to dent Milan's confidence to the extent that he ordered no further attacks on convoys in Legion-controlled territory. The arrival at Puebla of the cannons from the convoy that 3rd Company had sought to protect was decisive.

Assailed by heavy artillery, the fortress fell on 17 May leaving the road to Mexico City was open. Maximilian was enthroned the following month, but the war continued for four more years. The Legion continued to face the problems presented by guerrilla warfare in which a mobile enemy with considerable local knowledge attacked when he held the advantage. The Legion's cavalry became of great importance in this form of warfare, being used as a means to assist units that had run into difficulties. In March 1866, the cavalry was called upon to rescue 44 legionnaires who had been forced to barricade themselves into a church. In July, the cavalry prevented another Camerone by riding to the aid of 125 legionnaires who had barricaded themselves in a farmhouse near Matehuala, and spent two days fighting off attacks by over 500 Mexicans before the cavalry arrived and put the enemy to flight.

Although the cavalry were decisive in such engagements, the Legion's reputation was such that the Mexicans proved reluctant to attack a position known to be defended by legionnaires. However, the Mexicans were far more skilled at mobile warfare,

and on 15 June 1866 a convoy of Austrian troops and Mexicans loyal to Maximilian was attacked near Camargo. The Austrians fought bravely, but their cause was undermined when the two battalions of Mexicans changed sides in the middle of the battle. The Austrians were forced to surrender. Over 1000 prisoners were taken by the Mexicans, illustrating how difficult ultimate victory in Mexico would be.

The End in Mexico

By 1866, Napoleon III's idea of gaining influence in Mexico was in serious danger. The war was becoming increasingly unpopular with the French public, while the Legion began to suffer from large numbers of desertions. In December 1866, Napoleon III ordered the withdrawal of all French troops, with the last Legion unit leaving for Algeria on 18 February 1867. Napoleon III was not totally ungrateful for the Legion's efforts in Mexico. As a sign of his respect for the Legion, he ordered that the word 'CAMERONE' and the names of Captain Danjou, and Lieutenants Vilain and Maudet be inscribed in gold on the walls of Les Invalides in Paris. He awarded the Legion a battle honour for Camerone, and the date of the sacrifice made by a small party of legionnaires is now one of the key dates in the Legion's year, commemorated with great ceremony. The Legion's reputation was further enhanced, and its reputation for a willingness to fight against heavy, if not impossible, odds was born.

Legionnaires would have plenty of opportunities to ensure that this

Right: A weary and laden legionnaire pauses for a rest during the Franco–Prussian War. The desperate situation led to the Legion being employed on French soil for the first time. Although the Legion gave a good performance, the Prussian forces were far superior to those of France, and the war ended in a humiliating peace settlement.

reputation was maintained in conflicts to come, beginning with its first deployment for use in France when the Franco–Prussian War broke out in 1870.

African Base

One of the most notable features of the Legion was the fact that it was not allowed to operate in France, despite being an integral part of the French Army. While this exclusion had been designed to protect the French state from the possible threat posed by foreign troops, by 1870 the Legion was far better established, and the threat to French security came from abroad, in the form of Prussia. Over the course of the next 75 years, the Legion was to find itself fighting on French soil more than once.

This development was all unforeseen, of course, in the aftermath of the Italian campaign. When the legionnaires were safely returned to their Algerian base, the French Government set about reducing the unit from 5000 to 3000 men. The reduction meant that the artillery and engineering battalions were disbanded, and many French legionnaires were reassigned to other French Army units.

Almost 1000 foreign legionnaires had their contracts ended prematurely as well. This was not good for morale, as might be imagined,

and things were made worse by the fact that Algeria had an appalling harvest in 1867. This forced the legionnaires to subsist upon hard-tack biscuits and the poor-quality meat provided through the military supply system – many alternative sources of food to vary the diet, previously readily available, disappeared. Even where there were alternative sources, the price of the food was such that the legionnaires were often unable to buy it.

For those soldiers who found themselves in austere outposts in southern Algeria, the poor food, hard work and harsh living conditions only added to generally low morale. It was not long before inspecting officers were complaining that legionnaires were resorting to drink, and funding their alcoholic habits by selling their equipment. Finally, a serious cholera epidemic broke out, and the Legion garrisons did not escape its depredations. The Legion also seemed to have a run of bad luck on its expeditions against insurgents in Morocco and Algeria. Bad weather decimated one column in April 1868, with conditions becoming so awful that 19 men committed suicide rather than continue (there were numerous other casualties, including fatalities).

The always changeable weather to be found in the Algerian mountains had a similar effect upon a punitive expedition in February 1869. The fact that life in the Legion was hard was well-known, and events in Algeria and Morocco only added to this perception. Many legionnaires fervently hoped for some variation from this grinding routine, but the source of escape was rather unexpected: war with Prussia.

Franco–Prussian War

The Franco–Prussian War (1870–71) had its origins in French concerns about the rise of Prussian power in Europe, and misconceptions in Paris about how the rightful place of France in continental politics could be maintained. One of the major concerns was that the German unification movement appeared to be growing in strength, and a unified German nation presented a major challenge to French political domination.

While the Prussian Army turned itself into a professional, modern army with rapid-firing artillery and advanced rifles, the French Army was notable for the problems it faced. Many young men from the wealthier classes evaded military service quite legitimately by paying a substitute to take their place. As the Legion had discovered, the army was underpaid and poorly equipped. Many of the units in France, without the regular exposure to combat that the Legion faced, were lacklustre in their training provision. For example, although the French Army had a good service rifle, many of its soldiers were quite unable to shoot accurately with it. Solving the equipment shortages was not easy, since the National Assembly refused to fund rearmament, as both sides of the political spectrum

---

Sidi-bel-Abbès

The Legion's first true home was at Sidi-bel-Abbès, an Algerian town 50 miles south of Oran. Despite the image of Legion bases as rough, inhospitable places, Sidi-bel-Abbès was in fact a reasonably green and pleasant place, and as the marshes outside the town were reclaimed, the incidence of disease reduced dramatically – however, there were occasional outbreaks of illness that laid low a sizeable proportion of the troops. The town developed into a prosperous European community, and a number of legionnaires retired there, often setting up businesses that catered for their former colleagues. The isolated nature of the place meant that there were some difficulties, not least the fact that the bored legionnaires often frequented the local hostelries. Drunken brawls were a fact of life and those on guard duty at the camp gates often had to deal with the return of large numbers of drunken soldiers. Despite these problems, by the start of the twentieth century, Sidi-bel-Abbès was very much the Legion's 'home'.

In the aftermath of the World War I, Sidi-bel-Abbès ceased to be so important, as much of the Legion moved to Morocco at the behest of General Paul Rollet. Despite his belief that the Legion need not be based in Algeria any longer, Rollet accepted the decision to leave 1 RE in the country and helped to develop the legend of Sidi-bel-Abbès as the Legion's 'holy city'. The Legion retained a presence there until the 1960s, when Algerian independence required the removal of all French troops from the former colony.

Above: French and Prussian soldiers clash at the Battle of Mans-Champagne in the depths of a French winter. The contrast between French and Prussian uniforms is notable: the French wear clothing that differs little from that seen in portraits from the early part of the nineteenth century, where bright colours predominate: the Prussians, meanwhile, wear field grey and dark blue, making them less conspicuous on the modern battlefield.

were against such a measure. Finally, many of the senior officers had not appreciated the fact that war in 1870 would be very different from that fought in the Napoleonic era, or even Crimea. Cavalry charges, flair and an offensive spirit were the means by which the French Army would fight its battles, while artillery and good training (supported by rigorous staff work) would underpin the Prussian war machine.

All of the above was academic so long as France and Prussia simply regarded each other with mistrust rather than hostility. Events ensured that this situation changed. Once again, the source of the problem was Spain. Queen Isabella (the very same queen for whom the 'old' Legion had been sacrificed four decades before) and her mother Queen Maria Cristina, were driven into exile by the Spanish Army.

The wily Prussian Chancellor, Otto von Bismarck, took the opportunity to nominate Prince Leopold of Hohenzollern-Sigmaringen as the next Spanish king. This alarmed Napoleon III, who envisaged France being attacked by the Prussians from the Iberian peninsula as well as from the east.

French protests were, in fact, sufficient to see Leopold gracefully withdraw from consideration, but Napoleon III was not wise enough to leave the matter at a mere protest. He ordered the French ambassador to Prussia to make demands of the Prussian Government, which as well as insisting that Leopold withdraw, included one which would see King Wilhelm give a solemn promise not to support Leopold's nomination for the Spanish crown under any circumstances. The king, perhaps not unreasonably, told the French envoy that he would not accept being dictated to. On the same day, Leopold publicly announced that he had decided to withdraw his nomination (a decision that had been reached after the French had first shown displeasure). Wilhelm politely informed the French that the matter was now closed. Napoleon III disagreed, and ordered the ambassador to press the matter. Wilhelm refused to see the ambassador, and news of the diplomatic contretemps was released to the world in the form of a document drawn up by Bismarck. Bismarck phrased the document in such a way that it appeared that the ambassador had been treated with total contempt.

The French were outraged, but foolishly failed to ascertain from the ambassador whether this version of events was actually true. Within 24 hours of the news, the French Council of State had voted for war, and a day later, the National Assembly supported the decision while mobs roamed the streets of Paris calling for the Prussians to be punished for their temerity. War was declared on 19 July 1870, and the French Army was set upon the path to disaster.

The Disaster of 1870

The failings within the French Army were rapidly and ruthlessly exposed by the Prussians. The Legion, however, was not thrown into battle from the outset. The 1831 Law preventing the Legion from fighting on French soil was interpreted strictly, but this may have been because of the realization that a large proportion of the legionnaires were of German origin

– in 1866, a survey of nationalities had revealed that over 58 per cent of the men came from one of the German states. As a result, Napoleon III ordered the formation of a battalion of foreign volunteers separate from the Legion, only to find that the expected rush of eager recruits did not materialize. The Legion, meanwhile, found itself sent to replace *zouaves* (who could fight on the mainland) in a variety of insanitary garrisons. However, it was not long before the lack of foreign volunteers and the desperate need for troops changed the situation.

The foreign volunteers who had appeared were mustered into the 5th Foreign Regiment, which formed at Tours on 22 August 1870. Nearly 500 of the volunteers were German, and a number of Belgians also expressed their desire to fight against the Prussians. Both contingents presented the French Government with a problem – the Belgian Government was eager to maintain strict neutrality, and insisted that Belgian volunteers should not be allowed to fight.

To the volunteers' chagrin, they were sent to Algeria. The loyalty of the German volunteers was, of course, questionable, but the increasingly desperate situation confronting the French meant that it was decided that they should be employed. The 1831 Law was also to be ignored, and arrangements were made to send two of the four Legion battalions in Algeria to France, although the German members of those units were to be left behind.

These arrangements were largely academic as far as the outcome of the war was concerned. The

Prussians and their allies (Bavaria, Wurttemberg and Baden) suffered a brief reverse on 2 August when the French took Saarbrucken, but followed this up with a series of victories, culminating in the battle of Sedan. Napoleon III and 83,000 of his men were forced to surrender on 2 September, while the fortress of Metz was under siege. The result was a coup in Paris.

Napoleon III, in the hands of the enemy, was declared deposed, and the Third Republic was proclaimed. The Government of National Defence, recognizing the parlous situation that the whole of France was in, began erecting fortifications and establishing *ad hoc* army units in an effort to hold the Prussians back. It is to their credit that they managed to impose some semblance of order amongst French ranks to the extent that the Prussians were denied outright victory for another four months.

The Legion was called upon to play its part in this resistance. The 5th Battalion was sent to the front near Orléans, with the aim of holding off a Bavarian division that was threatening the city. The defence had not started well, when rumours of an imminent attack by enemy cavalry had prompted some of the troops defending the city to flee. The Germans were intending to attack, but were in fact only advancing towards Orléans when the panic began.

The 5th Battalion was hurriedly sent in to bolster the defences, and had not long established its positions when the enemy attack began. The legionnaires managed to hold out for all of 11 October, but the enemy was too strong. Eight hours of bitter house-to-house fighting concluded with dispersed groups of legionnaires heading to the rear. They were soon to find themselves heading back towards Orléans, ordered to retake the city.

The Legion's two battalions from Algeria joined the survivors of the 5th Regiment as part of the Army of the Loire, and prepared to attack. Recapturing the city was of critical importance, since doing so would permit the Army of the Loire to advance towards Paris, which was now under siege by the invaders.

Legion to the Fore

The two sides met at Coulmiers on 9 November 1870. The Legion was given the task of spearheading the French attack, and did the job well. Some of the momentum of the assault was threatened when other elements of the French force scattered under opposition, but the weight of the French attack was sufficient to persuade General Ludwig von der Tann, commander of the German forces, that he should withdraw. The retreat was carried out on 11 November, and it seemed as though the Legion had played a major part in winning a victory that would enable the relief of Paris.

Unfortunately for the French, the scale of the victory was not as great as assumed; von der Tann had been given orders to leave Orléans and move into the surrounding countryside if it appeared that he was facing a numerically superior French force. The clash at Coulmiers proved this, and von der Tann had no hesitation in removing his forces, who remained in good order as they left.

In fact, French hopes had already been dashed by events at Metz. The great fortress surrendered on 27

The Paris Commune

The surrender of Paris left the city without political direction, and this vacuum was quickly filled by political activists under the auspices of the Commune. The French Government, now at Versailles, called upon the Legion to assist in regaining control of the capital city. The Legion's ranks were bolstered with French troops, and as Douglas Porch has observed 'the Foreign Legion had never been less foreign'. The newly strengthened force joined with other units loyal to the Versailles government and set about besieging the capital. By 15 April 1871, legionnaires were fighting their way through the western outskirts of the city, and four days later captured three cannon after storming through a number of barricades.

The legionnaires were then withdrawn for a well-deserved rest. Although casualties had been high, the legionnaires were in good heart, not least because the Versailles government had been particularly generous in paying them, to ensure that there was no question over their loyalty. By the third week in May, the Legion was in the thick of the fighting again, helping to clear the last of the Communards from the city. As they fought their way through, the brutal nature of the fighting manifested itself in the shooting of many prisoners.

Although the Legion regimental diary records the shootings with a note of regret (and classified them as executions of traitors), this was not enough to stop the Legion's behaviour from being questioned later. The incidents did little to enhance the Legion's standing, apparently confirming its reputation for brutality amongst a significant number of Frenchmen. This ensured that the basing of the Legion in France was something that would not be countenanced by French governments for some time to come. Such was of little importance, however, since the very same governments had much for the Legion to do. Anxious to regain its standing after the humiliation of 1870, France set out to increase its colonial possessions – and at the forefront of this effort stood the Foreign Legion.

October 1870, freeing some 200,000 German troops for the siege of Paris. The Army of the Loire, buoyed by its success at Coulmiers, marched towards the capital, only to be defeated by a German counter-attack.

The French were driven back towards Orléans, and the legionnaires were tasked with serving as a rearguard for the French force in the second battle for the city on 4 December. They performed their task well, but the cost was high. The weight of the enemy attack was such that the Legion battalions found themselves split up into relatively small groups. Some did not receive the final order to withdraw, and were rounded up by the Prussians. In the bitterly cold weather, a number of legionnaires

Above: A ceremonial parade at the Legion's base at Sidi-bel-Abbès in 1906. The Legion's colour is being decorated with the insignia of the Legion of Honour, awarded to the Legion in recognition of its distinguished service since its formation in 1831.

died of hypothermia after being forced to sleep in the open. They were short of food and winter clothing and found that a number of local mayors were less than helpful in providing food or firewood. By the morning of 6 December 1870, the Legion had lost around 50 per cent of its strength, and the remnants of three battalions were formed into a single battalion.

Aware that the Legion had been amongst the best troops in the recent battles, the government arranged for 2000 new recruits to be sent to join the battalion, a step that was born of hope and desperation. Many of the new recruits had no idea of how to fire a rifle, and their military skills were decidedly lacking.

Although the Legion's more experienced soldiers (many given rapid promotions so that they could command the new arrivals) attempted to provide some training, this was insufficient. Furthermore, the failure of the supply system to provide food and clothing, coupled with the poor weather and generally low morale, meant that discipline began to crumble, even in more proficient units like the Legion. Desperate for food, legionnaires would leave their posts on hunting expeditions. These caused panic and confusion on more than one occasion, with rifle shots aimed at wildlife being mistaken for the opening of a Prussian attack.

Early in January 1871, an entire Legion battalion was taken prisoner without a shot being fired. Since no sentries had been posted all the men were sitting around a large camp fire when the Prussians arrived. Most seriously, however, the new arrivals to the Legion's ranks were ill-disciplined. There were complaints that some fought amongst themselves, but were rather less prepared to show similarly aggressive spirit towards the enemy. It was clear that the French position was irretrievable, and Paris surrendered on 28 January 1871.

Peace terms were formally agreed a little over a month later. On 6 March, all foreign volunteers who had joined the Legion for the war with Prussia were demobilized, along with all Frenchmen who had enlisted prior to 1863. This was not quite the end of the war for the Legion, however.

The Colonial Era: The Legion 1871–1914

The disastrous failure of French arms in the Franco-Prussian War cost France both territory and prestige. In a bid to recover from the stunning blow inflicted by the Prussians, and to offset the creation of a unified Germany that followed the war, the French Government began to cast covetous eyes on territories overseas, viewing the creation of a new empire as a useful means of regaining lost pride and status.

Algeria was already under French control, and in the decade after the end of the Franco-Prussian War, Senegal, New Caledonia, Tahiti, the New Hebrides and parts of Indo-China came under French authority, shortly followed by Tunis. Then Formosa and Madagascar fell to the French in 1885, Dahomey in 1892, part of Sudan the next year, and finally, in 1907, Morocco – where the Legion had already seen service – was added to the empire. This vast expansion of French terri-

tory ought to have placed the Legion at the forefront of operations, but for 10 years the Legion found itself used in non-combat roles.

While the building skills of the Legion, put to good use in Algeria in years gone by, were useful in establishing infrastructure, the lack of action was not particularly popular amongst legionnaires.

The situation began to change with the appointment of François de Negrier as commanding officer. De Negrier was one of the few men to escape from Metz after its surrender to the Prussians, and was much-loved by the legionnaires (despite his unwillingness to tolerate drunken misbehaviour). He concluded that the Legion needed to develop its mobility if it was to become a major fighting force again. The Legion already had something of a reputation for marching long distances (and has not lost it yet), but the practicality of expecting men to march swiftly across deserts and similarly inhospitable terrain while enduring harsh climactic conditions and carrying a large rucksack was limited at best.

De Negrier solved this problem by the simple expedient of introducing mules to the Legion. The legionnaires, equipped with their rifles, canteens and belt kit, could march much more easily alongside the mules, who carried the heavy equipment with little difficulty. Two legionnaires were assigned to look after each mule; when the going was good, the mules would carry one of the pair as well as the kit of both men. After a certain distance had been travelled, the mounted legionnaire would swap places

with his partner. The new formula soon proved an ideal way of ensuring that soldiers could dominate large areas of territory, enabling them to deal with hostile local tribes in a most effective manner. It made gaining control of the Algerian desert an easier task, and did much to raise the importance of the Legion in the consciousness of French politicians.

Although the Legion's later reputation was based heavily upon its presence in Algeria, one of the most significant elements of the Legion's work took place not in the desert, but in the jungles of Indo-China.

Indo-China

French interest in Indo-China began in the 1840s. Britain's acquisition of a base at Hong Kong in 1841 caused some concern in Paris, since it seemed that this would give strategic advantage to a long-time opponent of France. As a result, the French Navy began to search for a suitable location for a base of their own. The chance to obtain the base came in 1857 when the Second Opium War began.

Ironically, the French found themselves working alongside the British, occupying Canton and then, in 1860, Peking. It was noted that the Annamese (then the generic term for those living in what is now Vietnam) were vigorous in persecuting Catholics, and this offended French sensibilities. In 1858, Da Nang was bombarded, and the next year, a French force seized Saigon. These acquisitions were followed by the annexation of Cochinchina in 1867, and its assimilation as a French colony. By May 1884 French troops had forced the

Annamese to accept full French control through a 'treaty of protection' and had successfully compelled the Chinese to withdraw from Tonkin. The Chinese, who regarded Annam as a vassal state, were less than impressed with French efforts, and reacted strongly. A French force sent to occupy Lang Son was stopped with heavy casualties. The French Government was unimpressed, and decided that the time had come to bring the Indo-China problem to an end. A full invasion was planned, and the Legion was to play a major part. The French plan was to gain a decisive victory over China, but what emerged from the planning process was not destined to enter the annals of military history. For reasons that are not altogether clear, the French chose to invade Formosa in October 1884.

The attacking force landed relatively easily, but discovered that the Chinese had reinforced their garrison. The attack stalled, and casualties mounted as a result of Chinese action, monsoon conditions and a cholera epidemic. The declining French force was bolstered by the despatch of legionnaires in January 1885.

The new arrivals set about the Chinese with a will, and began to make progress, but it soon became clear to the high command – much later than it should have done – that the Formosa effort was unlikely to deliver the victory that would force the Chinese out of Indo-China.

Tonkin

The Chinese response to a build-up of French forces in Tonkin was to send three columns, each around 20,000 strong, to face the threat. In October 1884, some of these men surrounded the town of Tuyen Quang. A month later, 700 legionnaires and marines fought their way though enemy positions and reached the town, putting the Chinese to flight.

The legionnaires departed on 23 November, leaving behind a garrison made up of two companies of legionnaires, another company of local troops and a variety of men from support units. However, once the column that had opened the way for the garrisoning troops left, the Chinese returned and surrounded the town. The Chinese clearly intended to retake Tuyen Quang, but had not considered the fact that the legionnaires would resist, despite being vastly outnumbered. In addition, the fortress

Left: Legionnaires clash with Chinese troops besieging Tuyen-Quan during January 1885. The Legion's action in defending the town for more than a month against overwhelming odds ranks alongside the action at Camerone, although it is far less well known. The town was eventually relieved at the beginning of March 1885.

housing the garrison was overlooked by a number of hills.

The Chinese set to work preparing to take the town, and launched an attack on the night of 26/27 January 1885. They set light to the small village before the garrison and charged towards the Legion's positions. They were repulsed with great vigour and were forced to reconsider their plans.

The Chinese decided that they would have to adopt a more methodical approach, and they set about constructing trench lines that would enable them to reach the fortress with some degree of protection from French fire. Their first target was a small blockhouse, but the legionnaires became suspicious. They ascertained that the Chinese had sunk mineshafts beneath the blockhouse with the intention of blowing it up. The French responded by withdrawing the troops who were holding the blockhouse, and then destroyed it with artillery fire so as to deny the position to the enemy.

The Chinese maintained the siege, which began to adopt something of a regular pattern. Chinese snipers tried to keep the legionnaires away from their firing positions as their engineering teams extended the trenches towards the walls of the fortress. On 3 February, one of the local soldiers slipped away from the garrison with the task of alerting Hanoi that Tuyen Quang was under siege.

However, five days later, the Chinese received artillery and began bombarding the fort. It appeared as though any relief column would arrive far too late to make a difference to the plight of the garrison. However, the Chinese found the legionnaires to be determined opponents. They eventually reached a position from which the mines could be dug beneath the fortress walls, and these were detonated on 12 February. The Chinese rushed forward, only to run into withering fire from the legionnaires. Three more attacks were driven back, and once the hole in the wall had been filled, the legionnaires launched an aggressive raid to drive the Chinese out of their most advanced positions.

This was not the end of the siege, however. The besieging force obtained heavy mortars and subjected the garrison to increased bombardment. On 22 February, a Chinese attack saw three holes blown in the fortress wall. The defenders kept the enemy at bay for several hours while the holes were repaired, and had to do the same the following day and then two days after that.

A night assault on 27 February took until dawn to defeat. By 1 March, the sounds of firing from the south suggested that a relief force was on its way, but the garrison was in no position to break out to meet it.

It seemed that all was lost the following day, since the Chinese increased the volume of fire directed at the defenders, who prepared for a last stand. The next morning, the garrison discovered that the Chinese had left in the night, since the relief column was almost upon them: the intensified firing had been a last defiant gesture before departure.

While the siege at Tuyen Quang ranks as one of the Legion's finest hours (if not well known outside the Legion 'family'), it was of little real significance in the war to conquer Indo-China, as it was not in a strategically important position, and could easily have been bypassed by the Chinese as they headed south.

The most important of the battles was at Lang Son, but, in a rather bizarre twist, the battle appeared to have ended in near disaster when, in fact, it marked the point at which victory was gained.

Lang Son

As the French advanced through Indo-China, they had driven the Chinese out of the country from Bac Ninh to Bac Le, and only the need to relieve Tuyen Quang had prevented an advance to Lang Son near the Chinese border. The arrival of two further Legion battalions in January 1885 gave the French commander, General Brière de l'Isle, sufficient forces to launch an offensive.

The advance began on 3 February, the French troops heading for the mountainous area that stood between them and their objective. After two days, the legionnaires ran into Chinese positions, and found themselves involved in fierce fighting. Their first efforts to carry the enemy positions were reasonably successful, but casualties were extremely heavy as a result of the tactics employed – frontal assaults against well-defended positions are rarely successful without bloodshed. One Legion company lost all its officers, and the senior surviving NCO had to take over. The losses were a cause of considerable concern, and tactics were changed. It was soon discovered that attacking the Chinese from the flank was a much more efficacious way of achieving the desired result; frequently, the Chinese left their positions with little more than token resistance.

After the initial battle, the French force moved on, and although the Chinese continued to resist the advance was swift. By 12 February, the Chinese positions at Bac Viay were cleared, and the next day Lang Son itself came into view. The defending troops pulled out, and it was not long before the tricolour

---

Pacification Tactics

The pacification operations in Tonkin were slow, arduous work for the legionnaires, who fought alongside marines and local troops, the *tirailleurs tonkinois*. One of the major difficulties came from the fact that the brigands were highly mobile, and trying to track them down in the jungle was a thankless task. Many Legion columns spent days trooping through the jungle trying to find their elusive opponents, before returning to their base without having found anyone. Eventually, in the early 1890s, tactics were changed, and smaller columns were introduced, which proved more mobile and more effective. However, they did not bring about a rapid change in fortune, since the enemy remained difficult to find. In addition, there was always the risk that the enemy would be assisted by Chinese troops, whose commanders were not averse to embarrassing the French.

flew over the town. Ten days later, a column left Lang Son for the nearby town of Dong Dang, and drove the Chinese out. This success left the French with the option of entering China should they so wish, since there was little in between them and the Chinese border. As the French intention was simply to occupy Indo-China, this move was not taken, not least since the risks involved in invading China itself appeared to be substantial. However, the French position soon changed.

However, on 24 March the situation began to unravel. The invasion had infuriated the Chinese troops, many of whom made solemn oaths that they would throw the French out of their country or die trying, and the events of 24 March were to demonstrate the degree of determination on the Chinese side. A force of 20–30,000 Chinese fell upon the French, who had little option but to retreat in the face of superior numbers. As night fell, the rearguard of the French force crossed back into Indo-China, stopping at Dong Dang. They then fell back to Lang Son, where a Chinese attack developed on 28 March.

The Legion had sent forward over 1500 men to join the force at Lang Son, and this did much to alleviate the situation there, with several Chinese attacks being thrown back. However, General de Negrier was wounded in the chest, and had to hand over command to Lieutenant Colonel Herbinger. Herbinger decided that the only sensible course of action was to retreat, totally unhinging the position of France in north Indo-China in the process. However, the Chinese were becoming con-

Above: Major Domine, the commander at Tuyen Quang during the siege. Domine led a skilful defence of the town, despite the odds and succeeded in keeping the Chinese out of the town even though there were occasions when breaches were made in the town walls. His persistence was rewarded with the arrival of the relief column, which forced the Chinese to disengage.

cerned. They misread the situation in Tonkin, and credited the French with more strength than they actually had, while an uprising in Turkestan distracted their attention as well. Finally, Japan was showing signs of aggression over Korea, and the Chinese felt that it would be as well to end their conflict with France. Despite holding the advantage, they signed a ceasefire on 4 April 1885, and this was followed in June by the Treaty of Tienstin, in which China surrendered all claims

African Adventures: Dahomey

The Legion was not only active in Indo-China. It also saw much action in Dahomey (now Benin) and Madagascar. The Legion was chosen to provide troops for these campaigns because it offered a body of tough, willing soldiers who were able to endure the hardships of colonial campaigns rather better than troops used to postings in metropolitan France.

The campaign in Dahomey was extremely difficult, not because the opposition troops were of an equal quality to the legionnaires – they were not – but because the savage conditions that confronted the troops imposed heavy casualties through disease, and because the terrain over which they had to operate proved particularly difficult for

campaigning. The decision to send a Legion battalion to intervene in Dahomey was taken in 1892, as part of the 'scramble for Africa', when Britain, France and Germany began adding African states to their empires. For the British, such moves were seen as a defence against the threat of France or Germany gaining the means of interdicting the supply route between Britain and India.

For the Germans, the move to colonization was a chance for their newly unified state to gain prestige. For the French, as had been the case in Indo-China, African colonies appeared to offer the opportunity to regain France's reputation as an important nation that had put the disasters of 1870 firmly behind her.

A 4000-man punitive expedition under the command of Colonel Alfred-Amédée Dodds was sent, with 800 legionnaires in the vanguard. Rather oddly, the expedition chose to move through the jungle on foot, rather than use boats to navigate up the river. Even more oddly, the soldiers marched along the banks of the Ouémé, hacking their way through the jungle at a painfully slow rate. After a week's hard slog, the legionnaires finally managed to obtain a ride upriver by boat, and reached the high ground overlooking the river and the village of Dogba.

Early on the morning of 19 September 1892, the legionnaires were surprised by a Dahoman attack, with the enemy making good use of the foliage and half light of dawn to mask their approach. Despite having been taken by surprise, the legionnaires rapidly formed a defensive position and, supported by their own artillery and shellfire from a gunboat, brought the Dahoman attack to a standstill. Several bayonet charges were put in, and the Dahoman attack began to lose cohesion before finally breaking. The legionnaires were appalled at the carnage that lay before them – over 100 attackers had been killed or mortally wounded. Fearing that the retreat might have simply been to allow a regrouping, Dodds ordered his artillery to fire into the jungle ahead of the French positions, with the aim of disrupting any attempt to reform the enemy line. When the bombardment had been completed, the legionnaires moved forwards to discover more dead or dying Dahomans. A representative of Behanzin, the Dahoman king, was sent to threaten the legionnaires that unless they agreed to peace, they would be slaughtered by a 12,000-strong force that was on its way to deal with them. The emissary was brusquely informed that the Legion was not going to give in to such threats easily, and sent on his way.

Opposite: A bugler sounds the charge as the Legion and other French units attack the Dahoman village of Apka on 14 October 1892. Despite the extremely difficult conditions in Dahomey, the French forces performed well, defeating their adversaries in a little less than two months.

Having established a fortified base, the expedition set off along the east bank of the Ouémé. Another battle followed at the village of Grede, when the column (with marines in the lead rather than Legion troops) was ambushed. In the ensuing battle, which lasted for four hours, the Dahomans again displayed considerable bravery, but were routed by the superior skill-at-arms of the French forces. The French continued their advance, fighting a series of short, sharp actions as they went. By 16 October, the harsh conditions, coupled with the strain of constant fighting, was having a seriously adverse effect on the men of the column, and Dodds took the decision to withdraw to allow his troops some respite. This break also gave Dodds the opportunity to prepare for more attacks on the Dahomans. A week later, another Dahoman emissary appeared to ask for peace, but Dodds' insistence that the Dahomans abandon their positions on the river Koto was rejected. Further fighting took place in early November as the French moved towards the royal city of Cana.

Then, on 3 November, the French attacked the city, taking it with heavy casualties on the Dahoman side. This was the final battle of the campaign, and Behanzin opened negotiations with Dodds. The French conditions were severe – an indemnity of 15 million francs, the establishment of a French protectorate, the surrender of all artillery and a large proportion of the Dahomans' arms, along with the insistence that a French force should occupy the capital, Abomey.

Behanzin agreed, but when the time came to hand over his arms and the indemnity demanded, the French were less than impressed: 5000 francs, 100 rifles and two cannon were all that materialized. It is possible that Behanzin did not fully understand what the French were demanding – local custom was for the payment of tribute to the victor, not unconditional surrender. Tired of the Dahoman king's apparent unwillingness to accept peace on French terms, Dodds deposed Behanzin and replaced him with his brother. The Dahoman campaign could be regarded as a great success for the Legion.

upon Tonkin. The pacification of Tonkin was to take some time. Although the Chinese had surrendered their claim to the region, the French still had to deal with bands of Chinese brigands, the so-called 'Black Flags' who had aided the Chinese war effort and who had no intention of allowing French ownership of Tonkin to interfere with their daily business.

This resistance led to a major change in the posture of the Legion. The large, set-piece battles that had characterized its history to date were replaced by low-intensity conflict in which French fighting columns were sent out to find the brigands. The operational aim was to remove the enemy from a series of strongpoints in the Tonkin highlands from which they carried out raids on local habitations.

The fighting continued for the remainder of the 1890s – small in scale, with the brigands quite content to commit atrocities and mutilate the bodies of dead Frenchmen, usually by decapitating the corpses and placing the heads on display. The Legion responded in kind, and offered a bounty for every head that belonged – or more accurately, used to belong – to a brigand. The local Annamese proved extremely adept at collecting the rewards, and the French added to the effort of dissuading the locals from joining the pirates by publicly executing any that were captured, and displaying their heads on poles.

This brutal conflict began to wind down towards the end of the 1890s as a combination of French pacification and better relations with the Chinese brought dividends. By 1900, Tonkin was quiet, with much

of the credit for this state of affairs going to the Legion.

The Disintegration of Morocco

By 1900, the Legion, which had begun its days in less than ideal circumstances, and which had been mistrusted by French politicians on all sides, was now regarded as an essential component in French military operations. It appeared that a secure future lay before the Legion, as a leading part of maintaining the French empire in Algeria, Morocco, Africa and Indo-China.

For just over a decade, this was true. From 1914, however, the Legion would find itself embroiled in another major conflict on French soil, a conflict in which it would add to its legendary reputation. However, before then, it had much work to do in North Africa. The colonial competition that characterized the 1890s was a manifestation of the increasing tension amongst the leading European powers, a situation that grew worse as the twentieth century began. While relations between Britain and France were reasonably amicable, those with Germany were a source of considerable concern to the French Government. The loss of Alsace and Lorraine as the result of the 1870 war had left considerable bitterness towards the Germans, and this meant that the chances of a conciliatory approach between Paris and Berlin over international disagreements were unlikely.

One remaining source of tension in North Africa was Morocco, which had been a site for Legion operations in previous years as Algeria was brought under French control. Despite the strong French involve-

ment in parts of Morocco, it was an independent kingdom. The monarchy was relatively weak, and large areas of the Sahara were controlled by local tribal leaders. The French became progressively concerned about the fact that these tribal leaders represented an obstacle to a peaceful, francophone climate in North Africa. By the early 1900s, it was clear that pacifying the area was necessary, prompting a French expedition to take control.

Naturally enough, the Legion played a major part in this. The French began their operation to pacify the local tribes with a major sweep through the Sahara in March 1900, taking control of the fortified town of In Rahr. In May, the *2e Régiment Etranger* (2nd Legion Regiment; 2 RE) was taking part in a sweep towards the oasis of Timimoun, helping to capture it on 7 May. The Legion's renowned stamina was vital: to participate in the operation, 400 men had marched over 563km (350 miles) from their base in temperatures of 48 degrees centigrade (118 degrees fahrenheit) in what little shade there was.

They then repeated the journey, taking a circuitous, zig-zag route (increasing the distance that had to be travelled), finally reaching their billets after a march of 1834km (1140 miles). Many of the legionnaires returned with their boots in tatters, shredded by the unyielding rocks that littered their route. Although these achievements were significant, they did not completely pacify the Sahara, and the Legion was to find itself involved in much fighting in the region for some time to come. Again, this was small-unit warfare

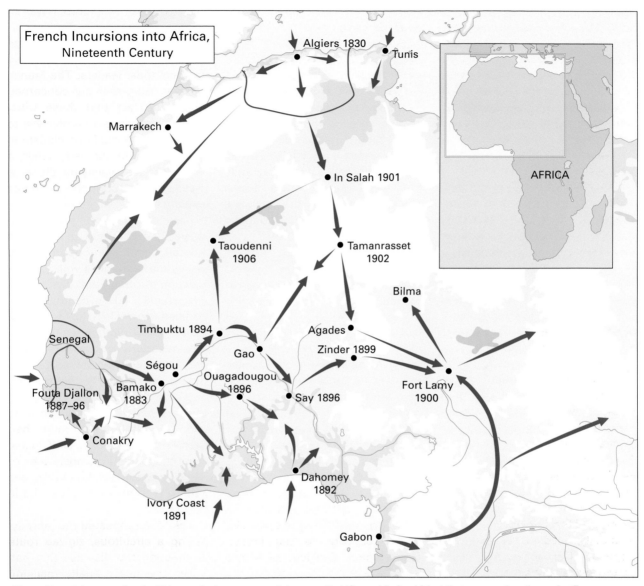

French Incursions into Africa,
Nineteenth Century

Algiers 1830
Tunis
Marrakech
In Salah 1901
Taoudenni 1906
Tamanrasset 1902
Bilma
Senegal
Timbuktu 1894
Agades
Zinder 1899
Gao
Fort Lamy 1900
Ouagadougou 1896
Say 1896
Bamako 1883
Fouta Djallon 1887–96
Ségou
Conakry
Dahomey 1892
Ivory Coast 1891
Gabon
AFRICA

Above: French intervention in Africa took place as part of the so-called 'Scramble for Africa' that occurred as the major European powers took control of key areas of the continent, seeking to deny their rivals an advantage. The Legion was heavily involved in gaining control of much of north-western Africa, advancing from its original bases in what was to become Algeria.

rather than grand pitched battles, and the tenacity of the legionnaires in difficult conditions was an enormous asset to the French cause.

Assassination and Retaliation

As a sign that the French were fighting a continuing battle to keep their North African possessions reasonably calm, on 1 June 1903 the governor of Algeria was assassinated. The French responded by sending a fighting column, including elements of 2 RE, into the area of Touat, where one of the French camps was attacked by 200 Berber warriors, a sign that unrest was increasing. In the middle of August, over 4000 tribesmen attacked a Legion position at Beni Abbès. The defences were bolstered by a platoon of legionnaires who arrived after a forced night march just prior to the battle beginning, acting on information that the tribesmen were about to attack. The garrison of 470 French and local troops managed to hold off the attackers for four days, at the end of which the tribesmen withdrew having suffered over 1200 casualties. The garrison lost nine men dead.

This was not the end of the fighting. At the end of August, a resupply column made up of 3000 camels and 2000 men was sent to provision isolated garrisons throughout Algeria. The column set out in three groups and the second of these was attacked on 3 September 1903. The legionnaires providing the escort for this group were taken by surprise, and the attacking tribesmen managed to stampede the animals, including the legionnaires' mules that were carrying water and ammunition. The legionnaires withdrew to two hillocks and set up a defensive position, while a small group of Spahis (local troops) were sent off to obtain help. The Berber tribesmen put in several attacks throughout the afternoon, inflicting casualties on both groups of legionnaires. Despite this, they were unable to break through the defences, although as the afternoon dragged on, it appeared that the legionnaires may well be forced to yield. As the situation became desperate, a bayonet charge succeeded in forcing the tribesmen back. As they regrouped, warily wondering what to do next, the relief arrived, including mounted infantry from 1 RE. At this point, the tribesmen fled, leaving the field to the legionnaires.

The battle had lasted eight hours, and only 32 of the original 113 legionnaires were unwounded; there were 36 dead. One of the dead was an experienced NCO, Corporal Tisserand, who had led the bayonet charge that forced the tribesmen back at a critical moment. In recognition of his service, Tisserand was given a posthumous commission. The Legion's tradition that a man promoted from the ranks must be sent to another regiment was maintained, and, rather bizarrely, the new Second Lieutenant Tisserand was posted to 1 RE.

The battle led the French Government to appoint Colonel Hubert Lyautey as the military commander on the border between Morocco and Algeria. Lyautey was given strict instructions that he was not to invade Morocco – and then promptly ignored them. On military grounds, Lyautey's disobedience was not unreasonable, since he was simply trying to ensure that he had the initiative. Lyautey did not want the fighting to take place on the lands inhabited by tribes that had come over to the French side, intending to demonstrate that the French intended to protect their new allies from the depredations of those who were not willing to abandon their opposition to French control in Algeria.

In addition, although the surviving documentation is unclear, it also seems very likely that Lyautey's insubordination was nothing of the sort. In April 1904, Britain and France signed the *Entente Cordiale*, and as part of the terms and conditions of this, it was agreed that if the Sultan of Morocco was unable to rule his territory, then the French should annex the country to ensure that the coastline was not suddenly open for a German intervention.

German Interference

The *Entente* was in the process of being negotiated as Lyautey began incursions into Morocco, establishing a series of Legion bases within the country, each about 160km (100 miles) away from one another. The French did not have to wait long for the Sultan to lose control of his country, for he was overthrown by his brother in 1908. The new ruler was sufficiently astute to recognize what was going on, and requested French military assistance. This prompted much outrage in Germany, and the Kaiser demanded an international conference to ensure that Morocco remained free of all outside influence (although what he actually meant was that he wished to ensure that German influence in Morocco remained as strong as it had been under the previous Sultan). The Algeciras conference did little to assuage German concerns, and gave France effective control of Moroccan security, plus approval for the movement of troops into the country to impose order and stability where this was required.

Gaining the desired stability was not easy. Within a matter of months, the French found themselves facing an awkward situation as Muslim zealots killed French dockworkers at Casablanca. The French response was to bombard the city and then send ashore a 3000-strong expeditionary force, including several hundred legionnaires, to ensure that Europeans living in the city were safe from attack.

Above: Legionnaires close with tribesmen in the Sud-Oranais. The Arab and Berber tribes proved difficult opponents, and it took a great deal of effort to subdue them. The Legion was often used as a back-up unit to mobile troops in this region, and this caused frustration as legionnaires found their time filled with much routine and little direct action.

Above: Legionnaires fend off an attack by Moroccan tribesmen. The Legion found the enemy cavalry a formidable opponent, but as illustrated here, if there was time to form a defensive square, the cavalry were usually unable to break the Legion's lines. Where Arab cavalry achieved an element of surprise, however, they inflicted several reverses on the Legion.

The number of troops had to be increased to meet the scale of the unrest, and by early 1908, there were 14,000 men based in and around Casablanca. The situation was not helped by events in September 1908, when the German consulate at Casablanca attempted to help three German legionnaires to desert along with three of their colleagues. Unfortunately, the deserters were spotted in the company of the German consulate's chancellor, and to make matters worse, the chancellor helped the six deserters into a rowing boat. This promptly capsized, and as the men stumbled ashore, they were surrounded by a small party of French sailors. A scuffle ensued, in which the German chancellor was involved.

This farcical incident had much wider repercussions: the Germans demanded that the three German deserters be released and that the chancellor (and his Moroccan bodyguard) be compensated for the indignity that they had suffered. The French refused, at which point Crown Prince Wilhelm, the heir to the throne, demanded that the 'insolent' French be taught another military lesson.

Although the German Government, and the Kaiser, were more sanguine about the affair (politely informing the Crown Prince that war with France would inevitably mean war with Britain), it demonstrated just how tense relations between the French and Germans were, with even the smallest perceived slight having potentially serious ramifications.

While the diplomatic farce over the Legion deserters was playing out, there were more serious issues for the Legion to deal with. The new Moroccan sultan was deeply unpopular, and three years after taking the throne found himself besieged in his palace at Fès. He appealed for French help, and in May 1911 a Legion-dominated column was sent to help. Elsewhere, a company from 1 RE was massacred in an ambush on the Algerian border, while other tribes rose up against the sultan.

Although the sultan was under the protection of the French, his country was in the process of disintegrating as the tribes sought to carve out their own land, fighting each other in the process. The sultan, well aware of the fact that he had lost control of the situation, invited the French to restore order in his country in March 1912, adding Morocco to the list of French colonies.

The Moroccan people were unimpressed, and vented their anger by joining in the general uprising. Lyuatey, now a general, was placed in charge of the pacification efforts as the French Resident in Morocco. Within two years, Lyautey was talking of his Legion troops as his 'most cherished soldiers' and the mainstay of his efforts to keep Morocco under control.

However, it was not long before many of his 'cherished' troops were to leave Morocco for the serious business of a world war. When the

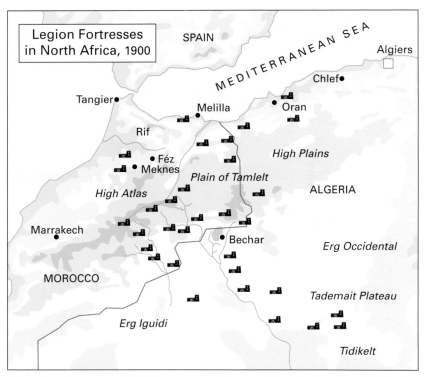

Above: In order to control the Moroccan and Algerian tribes, the French established an array of fortifications from which patrols and punitive expeditions could be launched. Conditions in the forts were often extremely basic, with punishing heat, disease and the vigorous efforts of the tribes proving a deadly combination for many legionnaires.

Above: General Lyautey, the Resident-General of Morocco, dines with Sultan Mulai Yussef. Lyautey, a prominent supporter of the Legion, had to strike a delicate balance in trying to maintain peaceable relations with local leaders and responding firmly to any challenges to French rule.

final efforts to maintain peace in Europe failed, the French Government instructed Lyautey to provide 40 battalions of troops for employment in France.

These included almost of all of his legionnaires. He was left with two battalions, made up entirely of Germans and Austrians who had taken up the French Government's offer of placing them in a position where they would not have to fight their fellow countrymen in the conflagration to come.

World War I

The outbreak of World War I prompted much enthusiasm in France and beyond. Many foreigners, outraged by the German attack on France, or perhaps seized with some of the romantic notions that were still associated with warfare, flocked to France and volunteered for the Legion. These included men who were well over military age, and those from decidedly nonmartial professions. Doctors, lawyers, teachers, academics, poets, writers and musicians all flocked to the ranks, along with a large number of Americans (including Cole Porter) who feared that they would miss the most exciting world event for years if they did not throw in their lot with the Legion.

By 1918, the Legion had received no fewer than 44,000 volunteers. To give some idea of the significance of the figures involved, the number of volunteers was four times higher than the Legion's overall strength in 1913. The Legion dealt with this massive influx of men by establishing new *régiments de marche* and placing these formations in the Moroccan Division – part of the Army of Africa of which the Legion was a part. The new regiments were made up of a mixture of volunteers and the experienced men sent over from North Africa.

Another of the regiments was a little different from the others in that it drew upon the men of the Paris fire brigade (which was, and still is, a military formation). Perhaps the most notable feature of all these formations was just how many of the NCOs in the Legion were Germans or Austrians. Despite the fact that their homelands were fighting against the French, the notion of 'the Legion is my country' was very much alive in these men. Furthermore, although capture by their countrymen would have almost certainly led to their execution as traitors, they were all prepared to take this risk.

The Legion was subjected to some reorganization in 1915, and the number of battalions on the Western Front went down from 16 to three as the need for troops in other theatres of war increased. After the reorganization, five more battalions were stationed in Morocco, three in Indo-China, two in Algeria and another in the Middle East (where they fought against Turkish forces).

This reassignment of forces, however, came only after notable

Marshal Hubert Lyautey

Hubert Lyautey attended the French military academy at St Cyr in 1873 and was commissioned as a cavalry officer in the following year. He saw service in Indo-China, Madagascar and Algeria, three theatres that brought him into close contact with the Foreign Legion. He made much use of the Legion after his appointment as Resident-General in Morocco in 1912. He was recalled to Paris in December 1916 to become War Minister in Aristide Briand's government, but resigned in March 1917 when he was unable to prevent Briand from agreeing to General Nivelle's plans for an offensive on the River Aisne. Lyautey surmised that the attack would be a disaster, and his resignation brought down the government. It did not stop the offensive, however, which proved to be the complete failure Lyautey had predicted.

Returning to his old position in Morocco, Lyautey remained in office until his retirement in 1925. During the remaining seven years of his tenure, Lyautey continued to employ the Legion aggressively, but became concerned about the level of desertion from its ranks, prompting him to issue an instruction that Legion units should never be employed alone as the reliability of some legionnaires could no longer be counted upon. The crisis soon passed, but Lyautey remained slightly ambivalent about the Legion – on the one hand, he valued and respected its fighting qualities; on the other, he was uncertain about the loyalty of some of its members. Lyautey enjoyed a quiet retirement, dying aged 79 in July 1934.

fighting on the Western Front. The French Army suffered horrendous losses in the first weeks of the war, with the so-called 'Battle of the Frontiers' contributing a large proportion of the 305,000 casualties sustained in just two weeks. Another 100,000 fell dead or wounded in the defence of Paris. The Legion, however, did not participate to any great extent in the fighting. The *4/1er Régiment de Marche* was sent to face the

Germans at Verdun on Christmas Day 1914, while the *3/1er Régiment de Marche* disgraced itself with a breakdown in discipline that saw its disbandment.

It was not until May 1915 that the majority of legionnaires were to join the fighting in the trenches, but once they were committed, they added to the Legion's reputation in some of the fiercest fighting that was ever encountered by legionnaires.

Hill 119

The Legion was then called upon to repeat its performance at Vimy Ridge on 16 June, attacking near Souchez at the feature known as Hill 119. The hill was taken, albeit with casualties, and the Germans responded with an artillery barrage of such ferocity that the legionnaires had to retreat. Despite the heavy losses sustained in these two attacks, the Legion had won a great deal of praise for its courageous and aggressive approach to operations.

Unfortunately, this was rather tarnished by a series of incidents that reflected poorly on the unit. On 16 June 1915, Greek legionnaires in one battalion refused to attack, complaining that they had joined the Legion to fight against the Turks rather than the Germans. It was only a combination of the presence of Algerian troops armed with fixed bayonets and a vague promise of being sent to the Dardanelles that persuaded the Greeks to attack. Some started the assault, but ran away under shell fire, much to the disgust of other legionnaires. The Greek contingent misbehaved again during the next few days, and were sent away for further training.

In fact, they proved to be almost impossible to mould into disciplined soldiers, and the battalion was broken up. The events surrounding the Greek battalion helped to lower morale amongst other nationalities within the Legion, particularly the Russians. Many of the Russian legionnaires secured transfers to other regiments or even their own nation's forces, something that caused discontent amongst the legionnaires.

Despite these problems, the Legion continued to perform well when called upon. The opening of a French offensive in Champagne

Above: Legion gunners prepare to fire another shell as part of a bombardment during an action in the Middle East or North Africa (probably Syria). Artillery was often a decisive factor in the fierce fighting between the French and local insurgents.

Above: Troops on training exercises at around the time of the start of World War I. The French Army at this time was reasonably well-equipped, but its red and blue uniforms were hardly suited to the modern battlefield. Tactical skill was also rather lacking in many quarters, leading to heavy casualties in the opening battles of the war.

saw the Legion directed to attack the Butte de Souain on 25 September and then the German positions at Navarin Farm. In both instances, the Legion did particularly well, in one instance coercing would-be deserters from other French units back to their position. Although the Legion's attack on the farm proved to be unsuccessful and particularly costly, it provided a diversion that allowed other units to take the position by outflanking the German defenders, who were concentrating upon the fierce assault being put in by the legionnaires. The losses in the Champagne offensives marked the point at which the Legion had to be reorganized, however. Many of the foreign recruits from 1914 had been returned to their national armies or posted to metropolitan units. Many more were dead or unlikely to return to battle as a result of their wounds.

The Legion's strength had been close to 22,000 at the start of 1915, and had fallen to half this as 1916 arrived. Out of the 10,683 men in Legion ranks at this point, only 3000 were to be found on the Western Front. As Douglas Porch has observed, this was a temporary setback, since those who remained with the Legion after the restructuring were determined troops who set about transforming the unit from one that had gained a rather mixed reputation over the course of 1915, into one that was regarded as an elite unit only a short while later.

All Quiet

The reduction in the strength of the Legion at least enabled an increase in its efficiency, assisted by the fact that 1916 proved to be a quiet year for the formation. This lull may seem rather peculiar, given that the year was marked by the sanguinary battle at Verdun, where losses for the French and Germans were appalling, and by the battle of the Somme, where British and German losses were measured in the hundreds of thousands. Yet the Legion managed to avoid all this, and held a relatively quiet part of the line for much of the year. The only major action of note was actually in

support of the British offensive on the Somme. The Legion distinguished itself on 4 July 1916 when it was required to put in attack against Belloy-en-Santerre. The Germans had fortified the village, and it was likely to prove a challenge, but it was one the Legion rose to. The attack did not begin well, since artillery support was lacking, and the legionnaires were required to charge across 200m (656ft) of open ground. The German machine gunners inflicted a large number of casualties on the attackers, but did not manage to break up the momentum of the attack, with the second wave taking the sensible decision to approach on hands and knees.

Once they had gained sufficient cover, the second wave leapt to their feet and stormed into the village. Vicious house-to-house fighting took place over the next two hours, until the last of the Germans was driven out.

The legionnaires then dug in amongst the ruined buildings and waited for the inevitable German counter-attack. This soon arrived, but the legionnaires drove it off. The Germans were not to be dissuaded, however, and launched a whole series of counter-attacks designed to dislodge the Legion; however, all failed.

Opposite: Giving a sign of the often-remarkable nature of trench warfare, the legionnaires in this photograph are separated from the enemy by nothing more robust that the wall of sandbags that block the trench. The long rifles employed by the French Army often proved to be something of a handicap in fighting of this type, since they were not easy to handle in the confines of a trench.

On 6 July, fresh troops came up to Belloy-en-Santerre and relieved the legionnaires, who were able to go to the rear for a brief rest. Although the legionnaires took 750 German prisoners of war back with them, they had suffered heavy casualties once more: of just under 3000 officers and men who took part in the attack, over 30 per cent of them were killed, wounded or listed as missing. Despite the heavy losses, the legionnaires were proud of their achievements, and the battle remains regarded as being one of the most impressive in the Legion's history.

The legionnaires who returned on 6 July were given little more than a day to recover, since on the next day they were told that they would be attacking Chancelier. This was another hard task, and 400 more men fell in action. The losses

---

Vimy Ridge

The first major commitment of legionnaires to operations came on 9 May 1915, when they were given the task of taking German positions on Hill 140, a feature on Vimy Ridge, near Arras. The attack was preceded by a huge bombardment that lasted for five hours. However, since much of the barrage was composed of shrapnel, it did little damage to the German wire. Just before 10:00, the guns fell silent and the countryside came alive to the sound of bugles as the signal for the advance. The first men reached the German wire and had to wait for colleagues with wire-cutters to make a path through. At this point, the German machine guns opened fire.

The casualties amongst the legionnaires increased as artillery fell upon them, and they ran forward towards the next array of enemy wire. More men fell, but the survivors still carried on, heading for the German positions. As they reached them, the Germans began to fall back, pursued by the legionnaires. The legionnaires moved through the trench positions, using grenades to clear the German strongpoints. Just as it seemed that the operation had been successful – and some legionnaires had gone beyond the German first-line positions and were on the outskirts of Vimy and Givenchy – shells fell on them. The legionnaires quickly realized that these were French rounds, and scurried for cover in the German dug-outs. The Germans gained a reputation for building particularly strong dug-outs during World War I, and these were no exception: the legionnaires remained safe from their own bombardment until it lifted some time later.

Although the first action had been a success, the Legion's losses were heavy. The Germans put in a counter-attack in the afternoon, and the greatly depleted Legion force had to retreat, giving up the 5km (3 miles) depth of territory that they had won at the cost of 50 officers and just under 1900 NCOs and legionnaires. The Legion's commanding officer, Colonel Theodore Pein, and all three battalion commanders were amongst the fatalities.

Above: French troops, including legionnaires, in the primitive conditions in the tunnels beneath the fortress of Verdun. The massive German assault there in 1915–16 saw much hand-to-hand fighting in the tunnels, with the troops enduring horrendous conditions as the advantage switched between the two sides.

meant that it would be difficult for the Legion to participate in any more action in the short term, and it was not, in fact, until 1917 that the Legion saw major operations again. It should not be thought that the Legion was under-employed during 1916, however.

Much of this crucial year of the war was taken up with holding relatively quiet sectors of the front, or in the rear carrying out training as new recruits to the unit were given some instruction in battle tactics and the opportunity to work with their new colleagues.

Return to Fighting

After a short respite in 1916, 1917 saw the Legion committed to the Nivelle offensives in April, part of a grandiose plan that was meant to win the war, but which in fact came close to shattering the French Army. After the lack of progress in

1916 (the defeat of the German assault at Verdun notwithstanding), the French and British governments wished to see a renewed effort to drive the Germans out of France and Belgium, and to bring about a peace settlement.

The Legion was to play a part in the opening of the offensive, putting in an attack on Aubérive on 17 April 1917. Despite a week-long bombardment, the German defensive bunkers were virtually untouched, and their machine guns exacted a heavy toll amongst the legionnaires. The plan in shreds, the Legion officers simply gathered surviving legionnaires around them, and instead began a slow and bloody infiltration of the village that took four days. The legionnaires fought their way through 11km (7 miles) of trenches as they went, slowly dislodging the Germans. Finally, on 20 April, the German reserve positions fell, and the village was taken.

The cost was high. One battalion had lost nearly 600 men, while the regimental commander was also amongst the fatalities. Once again, despite heavy losses, the Legion gained much credit for its determination and taking the enemy positions against formidable odds. It would appear that this determination was part of much-improved morale amongst the Legion in 1917, with its members gaining a sense that they were regarded as something of an elite formation.

This feeling of worth may explain why the Legion was not being engulfed in the mutinies that swept through the French Army as morale plummeted and soldiers began to complain bitterly about the way in which they were treated by the high command. About a third of the army refused to follow orders, and the Legion found itself with the task of sealing off roads to prevent desertions and, ultimately, returning the mutineers to the front.

The Final Year

At the end of 1917, the Russian Revolution had taken the Russians out of the war as the new Bolshevik government sought a peace treaty with the Germans. The Germans were able to transfer a large number of men to the west, enabling them to launch a massive offensive on 21 March 1918.

The spring offensives began with an incredible degree of success. All along the French and British fronts, the Germans broke through to depths far greater than any achieved at any other time in the war. The Legion, then holding the line in Lorraine, was pitched into the defence against the German attacks. On 26 April, the Legion was given the task of occupying Hangard Wood, just to the north of the road between Amiens and Noyon. The legionnaires attempted to advance in thick fog, and the confused nature of the fighting meant that the Germans were able to infiltrate into the French lines and cause considerable casualties amongst the advancing men.

The legionnaires were at least supported by artillery and British tanks, but the close-in fighting meant that artillery was difficult to employ, while the tanks provided some useful support, but not enough to prevent the Germans from breaking up the first attack after it had gone only a few hundred yards from its start point. A German counter-attack forced the legionnaires out of the wood, but they were able to retake it later. The day's fighting cost 325 dead or missing and 497 wounded. Despite the best efforts of the Germans, the Legion held the wood until it was relieved on 6 May, fighting off a number of German attacks. Although the German offensives were beginning to lose momentum, they were far from over.

On 27 May, the Germans attacked along the Chemin des Dames. Unfortunately for the French, the general commanding in that region had refused to believe reconnaissance reports from a Royal Air Force squadron that was assigned to the area for a rest. It had spotted movements suggesting that an enemy attack was imminent. No real preparations were made, and those that were placed a large number of French soldiers in the forward positions, where they suffered heavy casualties when the Germans demonstrated that the RAF squadron had not been making things up.

Firm Defence

The Legion was taken to the area by motor transport, along with the Moroccan Division, where they made their stand on 30 May. Although the Germans managed to make some inroads into the first line, they found that the main French position was impassable as the defenders put up stiff resistance. The Germans made a series of unsuccessful attacks, and were finally forced to switch to the defensive. Again, the Legion gained much praise for its firm defence, but this was achieved – once more – at the cost of heavy losses, many of them to enemy artillery and gas.

The losses, which ran to more than 1200 men, were not quickly replaced. This did not prevent, however, the recently appointed supreme allied commander, General Ferdinand Foch, from using the Moroccan Division (of which the Legion was a part) as the spearhead for his counter-attack on 18 July 1918, the date which is generally accepted as marking the end of the German offensives and the beginning of the final stages of the war. The Legion carried out a much-admired attack south of Soissons, over-running enemy positions with great alacrity and taking a large number of prisoners. The customary German counter-attacks were ineffective, and the Legion held on. However, yet more men were lost (nearly 800) and the Legion's commander, the much-loved (and slightly eccentric) Colonel Paul Rollet began to become concerned for the future of the Legion's units in France – it appeared that there was some danger of his running out of men before the end of the war.

Rollet's concerns were well-founded, but the reputation of the Legion was such that it was selected for another attack near Soissons, this time on 1 September. The plan was to pursue the Germans as they

Right: Legionnaires seen during the fighting in Hangard Wood in April 1918. The Legion was tasked with clearing the Germans out of the wood in an effort to blunt the enemy's Spring offensives. This was done at appalling cost – 1 RMLE lost all its officers and NCOs and was commanded by Legionnaire Kemmler until new officers and NCOs were sent forward to join the battalion.

Opposite: General Paul Rollet, the so-called 'father of the Legion'. Rollet joined the Legion as a young Lieutenant in 1899, serving first in Madagascar. As he rose to the top of the French Army, he acted as a patron for the Legion, formalising much of the Legion's heritage and tradition, most notably by making the commemoration of Camerone Day an annual event.

retreated. The fighting was hard, and although the Legion enjoyed considerable success, its losses were such that many of its companies were down to about 50 men by the end of the fighting. This was still not deemed sufficient reason to pull what was now clearly regarded as an elite unit out of the line, and the Legion was called upon to join the attack on the Hindenburg Line on 14 September. The gaps in its ranks notwithstanding, the Legion did well, breaking through the line and taking a substantial number of prisoners in the process. While the Legion continued to be involved in the fighting until the end of the war, breaking through the Hindenburg Line was its last major battle of the war. After a difficult start, the Legion had established a substantial reputation as an elite fighting force that was able to achieve objectives despite testing circumstances and heavy casualties. Although the figures are not entirely clear, it would seem that the Legion suffered 11,000 casualties in the course of the fighting on the Western Front.

The Legion's performance in World War I gave a clear demonstration of its value as an effective fighting force in modern warfare. However, with the war out of the way, the legionnaires were sent back to their pre-war duties of maintaining France's imperial position, with a return to colonial policing and taking on responsibility for the territories mandated to French control as part of the Versailles peace settlements. While on the surface the task may have appeared identical to that carried out in the pre-war era, there were subtle differences. New challenges would be presented over the next 20 years.

Colonial Warfare: 1918–1962

Following 1918, the Legion was notably different from the one that existed before the war. Thousands of displaced men from Russia, Austria, Hungary, Germany, Turkey and what had become Yugoslavia flocked to the recruiting offices, looking for a new home, which they found in the 'family' of the Legion.

Colonial operations continued in Algeria and Morocco from November 1919, when those elements of the Legion that had fought in France were returned to the base at Sidi-bel-Abbès and reconstituted as *3e Régiment Etranger D'Infanterie* (3rd Legion Infantry Regiment; 3 REI).

Over the course of the next three years, a regular pattern of operations in the desert was resumed.

General Paul Rollet

General Paul Rollet was born on 20 December 1875 in Auxerre, the son of a French Army officer. Rollet attended the French Military Academy at St Cyr, and on graduation, joined the 91st Infantry Regiment. However, bored at the lack of action, he transferred to the Foreign Legion in December 1899. He distinguished himself in Madagascar, Morocco and Algeria. Promotion took him away on other duties, but he returned to the Legion in 1917 as commanding officer. His irreverent attitude to his superiors and obvious personal courage (he refused to replace his képi with a helmet even during artillery bombardments) earned him the adoration of his men.

In the aftermath of World War I, Rollet took charge of rebuilding the Legion, and was largely responsible for the development of much of the Legion's tradition through the method of highlighting past actions and promoting knowledge of the unit's history: the most obvious manifestation of this was through the formalisation of Camerone Day as a key part of Legion ceremonial. His efforts ensured the survival of the Legion in the difficult years after the war, and did much to create a positive popular image of the unit that overcame some of the accusations levelled at legionnaires prior to the Great War.

The formal adoption of the white képi as the Legion's headgear was entirely a result of Rollet's lobbying the War Ministry. He retired in 1935, having made sure that his beloved Legion was a key part of the French armed forces, earning him the title of 'father of the Legion', even though his involvement came a little under a century after the Legion was actually formed.

Above: A unit of legionnaires pose for the camera somewhere in Morocco during the battle against Abd-el-Krim and the Rif Rebellion in the 1920s.

Fighting columns headed out into the so-far unconquered parts of the desert to take on the local tribesmen in the spring, with the fighting going on through the summer and autumn, before the legionnaires would occupy blockhouses and fortifications during the harsh winter. The hard conditions, ranging from extreme heat to extreme cold, coupled with the fact that the tribesmen were highly adept at ambushing small patrols, did little for Legion morale.

This was not helped by a notable reverse in 1929 when 41 legionnaires were killed at Djihani when they were ambushed. The killings caused consternation in France,

and the Legion was soon given a greater number of automatic weapons to enhance the firepower that could be used against the tribesmen. Another new feature of Legion operations was brought about by fresh fighting in Morocco. A Spanish force was wiped out by Moroccans led by Abd-el-Krim, a man who proved far more astute than many of the opponents that the Legion had faced in the region to date.

His victory over the Spanish, which came at Anual in 1921, was spectacular. Over 12,000 Spaniards were killed, and their weapons and ammunition were taken. General Lyautey was concerned and asked

Paris for reinforcements, but all that emerged was the creation of a *Régiment Etranger de Cavalerie* (REC). While the establishment of a horsed cavalry regiment seemed something of an anachronism, even allowing for the context of operations against rebels in the desert, this represented an important development and the Legion becoming an even more versatile force. It was to play an important part in operations in 1925, when el-Krim crossed into French Morocco with 30,000 warriors.

Morocco and Syria

The vast force of rebels that swept into Morocco represented a serious threat to the French position, not least since it appeared that el-Krim intended to oversee the creation of a 'Rif Republic' in Morocco. Lyautey's request for reinforcements was shown to be a sensible one, but it was too late to do anything to stop the inexorable advance of the enemy.

The rebels were being advised by a Legion deserter, Joseph Klems. They used his expertise to avoid frontal assaults on Legion outposts, instead bypassing them with the main body of the rebel force, which headed for the Moroccan capital while leaving behind a small besieging group to take the French forts. The legionnaires fought in an array of desperate last-ditch stands. Within 10 days, el-Krim's forces were on the outskirts of the capital, Fèz. For reasons that are unclear, he then paused before trying to launch an assault to take the city, which gave the French the opportunity to send 50 battalions to Morocco.

They also sent Marshal Philippe Pétain, the hero of Verdun, to replace the unfortunate Lyautey, made a scapegoat for the failure of the politicians to listen to his pleas for more men. Incredibly, el-Krim failed to do anything for a year, and this gave the French the opportunity for which they were waiting. Pétain launched a massive offensive on 8 May 1926, driving the Rif forces back to where they had come from. Eighteen days later, el-Krim surrendered.

It was, however, another seven years before the last of the rebels surrendered, with the Legion playing the leading part in defeating the remaining bands of rebels. The Legion's efforts were aided by the provision of motorized

Above: Legionnaires set out on patrol in the Sahara on 7 January 1928. The photograph provides excellent detail of Legion dress in the desert, which contrasts with the stylised paintings seen earlier in this section. Note that the white képi cover is worn only by the legionnaires, and not the senior NCO leading the patrol.

sections, which made movement across the desert much swifter (if more complicated by the demands of the vehicles as opposed to horses).

The Legion faced other problems in Syria. A rebellion in 1925 saw an attempt by Druze rebels to seize the town of Messifré, which was defended by a combination of 4 REI and 1 REC. A bitter battle took place on 16 September, in which the Druze lost over 500 men in their failure to take the town.

Such events were common in Syria, maintaining the continuity of Legion operations in French colonial possessions – although the men and equipment changed from year to year, the basic principles did not. The legionnaires carried out patrols against rebel tribesmen, and faced the risk of the occasional rebellion. However, both Syria and Algeria were relatively quiet from 1927 until the outbreak of World War II. The period, therefore, was

Above: Taken in June 1925, this photograph shows legionnaires and local troops in action during the capture of Astor Hill in Algeria. The fighting took place as part of a French advance towards Sker as rebellious tribesmen were being dealt with once again.

Above: Although not showing Legion troops, this photograph gives a good idea of the nature of mounted troops employed on colonial policing duties alongside the Legion. These are Spahis, led by French officers and NCOs.

marked by small-scale actions that received little press attention, and which appeared to demonstrate that the French empire in North Africa and the Middle East would continue without challenge for some time to come. Everything was to change in 1940.

World War II

The outbreak of World War II on 3 September 1939 did not instantly presage major fighting in Europe. The so-called 'Phoney War', however, was demolished when the Germans invaded France and the Low Countries on 10 May 1940. The campaign was brief, and ended with French capitulation on 22 June. The German victory left the Legion in a state of limbo, for while France was now under German control, the French colonies were not. The establishment of the collaborationist Vichy regime brought some clarity to proceedings, leaving the colonies under French control. Even now there were complications, with the creation of the Free French forces.

The Legion found itself in the unenviable position of fighting on both sides, as most legionnaires in the now-neutral colonies remained under the Vichy regime, while others joined de Gaulle's Free French.

The most prominent legionnaires in the Free French forces were those from the *13e Demi-Brigade de Légion Etrangère* (13th Legion Demi-Brigade; 13 DBLE) which, by a quirk of fate, was in Scandinavia in May 1940, fighting as part of the forces committed to the Norwegian campaign.

The Allied withdrawal from Norway coincided with the French

capitulation, and 13 DBLE found itself in Britain when de Gaulle announced the formation of the Free French.

About half of the legionnaires decided that they would continue their journey to Morocco, but the remainder decided to remain with the Free French forces. The men of 13 DBLE who decided to join de Gaulle were to provide the nucleus of the Free French forces in Britain. And it was not long before 13 DBLE would be engaged in opera-tions against Vichy French possessions.

Legionnaire versus Legionnaire

In 1941 13 DBLE was part of an Allied expedition to take control of Syria and Lebanon, which placed it in the unfortunate position where it could be forced to fight against other Legion units. For this reason, the British did not make great use of the Legion in the capture of Damascus, or, for that matter in Lebanon – on the other side, however, 6 REI put up stiff resist-ance, but was eventually forced to capitulate.

When the surrender was taken, the British offered all French sol-diers the choice of returning to Vichy or joining the Free French. A total of 32,000 went to France, and 692 legionnaires decided to join the side that they had only just finished fighting.

The 13 DBLE played more of a part in the fighting in North Africa, when it won a notable victory against the Afrika Korps at Bir Hakim in 1942, shortly before the major British victory at El Alamein and the subsequent invasion of North Africa by an Anglo-American force (Operation Torch).

This prompted the Germans to occupy Vichy France, changing the situation for the Legion once again. With the North African colonies firmly under Allied control by the middle of 1943, the Army of Africa (which included the Legion) put men at the disposal of the Allies, with most of its best troops being legionnaires.

The additional recruits to the Allied cause were re-equipped with British and American uni-

---

Famous Legionnaires

The Legion has attracted a number of men who went on to gain celebrity after their service; in one or two cases, the men were well-known prior to joining up. The most com-monly cited famous legion-naire in the English-speaking world is probably the song-writer Cole Porter (pictured), who joined the Legion in 1916 after the failure of his first Broadway musical *America First*. It is probable that Porter enlisted not so much because of disappointment at the failure of the project, but because he was yearning for adventure. He

served in North Africa before being commissioned and trans-ferred to an officers' training school in Fontainbleau, where he taught gunnery methods to American troops.

Other notable legionnaires included several members of European royalty. Prince Aage of Denmark (a cousin of the king of Denmark), searching for something to do after the bankruptcy of the banking business in which he was involved, spent 17 years as a Legion officer, where he was much admired by his men. His autobiography *My Life in the Foreign Legion* was highly acclaimed for its accuracy in portraying Legion life. Prince Amilakvari of Georgia gained a similar reputation for lead-ership, and was much mourned by his men when killed at Bir Hakim in 1942.

While the Legion may not be said to have produced many famous men, this is perhaps in part because many legionnaires have joined to keep a low profile, or to change the direction of their lives. They have not, therefore, gone on to seek fame or fortune, and remain recognized almost exclusively within the Legion family rather than beyond.

forms and weapons, giving them compatible logistics with the Allies, before being deployed to Italy in early 1944. After four months of fighting in Italy, the Legion was withdrawn to participate in the Allied landings in southern France (Operation Anvil/Dragoon).

The legionnaires thus fought in some of the battles to liberate their adopted homeland, ending the war in Austria on 6 May 1945. The confused situation affecting French forces in the European theatre meant that the war could not be regarded as a glorious chapter in Legion history, although the dogged, last-ditch defence of Bir Hakim stood out.

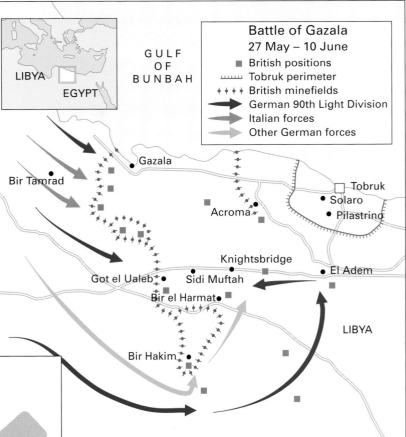

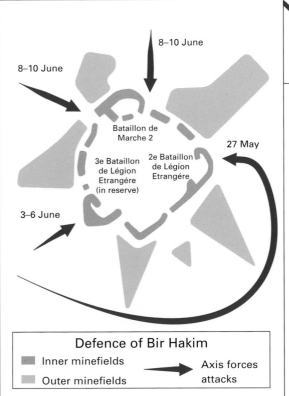

Above: The Foreign Legion's efforts at Bir Hakim were part of the wider battle of Gazala in May and June 1942. Rommel launched an assault with the intention of outflanking the Allied positions defending against a drive on the strategically important port of Tobruk. Situated on the extreme left flank, Bir Hakim was the most important position in the defensive line, held by the men of 13 DBLE, who were anxious to restore French honour after the debacle of 1940.

Left: The legionnaires at Bir Hakim faced a number of determined assaults by the Italian and German forces, but their defensive positions proved to be extremely difficult to attack, with minefields funnelling the Axis units' attacks into compact fire zones. However, a continuous series of enemy assaults brought increasing pressure on 13 DBLE, who were worn down by attritional force. As a result, 13 DBLE broke out from their positions on 11 June 1942. Although the position at Bir Hakim was lost, the defence was a success for the Legion, since it imposed serious delay upon Rommel's efforts to attack Tobruk.

Above: Legionnaires sprint across open desert during the Battle of Bir Hakim. The battle was a notable success for the Legion, and did much to cement the unit's reputation as part of the Free French forces fighting alongside the British and Americans.

Indo-China

During World War II, the Legion's units in Indo-China found themselves tolerated by the Japanese, the dominant power in the region, until March 1945. The Japanese concluded that the defeat of Germany was imminent, and that this would make the French, now allied to the Americans and British, eager to resume their colonial responsibilities in Indo-China, with all that this implied for the Japanese war effort. The Japanese therefore decided to occupy Indo-China, and did so despite vigorous resistance from the legionnaires garrisoning the country. Many were rounded up and executed, but some 3000 men from 5 REI marched to China.

They were ambushed on several occasions by the enemy, but fought their way through. There were only 1000 left when sanctuary was gained, but by the time they arrived the French Government had written the unit off. It was disbanded as soon as it returned to Indo-China.

The Japanese defeat in August 1945 left Indo-China in a parlous position. The local nationalist movement, the Viet Minh, written off by the French as something of an irrelevance, had time to mobilize and garner support for independence under its charismatic leader Ho Chi Minh. The Viet Minh had represented the only credible source of opposition to the Japanese during the war, and in the absence of the French, it established the Democratic Republic of Vietnam.

Tonkin to Dien Bien Phu

The French return to Indo-China began with the insertion of a small party of paratroops on 22 August 1945, preceding the arrival of the British force that was to take control of the country until sufficient French troops could be deployed. On 23 September, newly arrived French troops took over from the British, removed the Viet Minh government, and restored French colonial rule. A British diplomat noted that the uncompromising way in which the government was replaced was bound to provoke a reaction, and he was quite correct. Attempts were made at compromise, resulting in an accord between Ho Chi Minh and the French, who recognized the Vietnamese Republic as part of the French Union in return for Vietnamese respect for French interests. The French were allowed to base troops in North Vietnam, and thousands of these were legionnaires – 2 REI, 13 DBLE and 3 REI arrived in February 1946, just a month before the Accord was formally agreed. An uneasy peace persisted until November, when unrest broke into outright warfare. The conflict rapidly turned into a guerrilla war, with the Legion being employed to pacify the country. Under the command of General Jacques Leclerc, the French forces employed a method known as

Above: A light tank of the M3/M5 series moves forwards towards Ninh Hoa, supporting an attack against Viet Minh forces. The 37mm (1.4in) gun on the M3/M5 proved particularly useful as a fire support weapon, especially against Vietnamese wave assaults on French positions.

Above: Fresh-faced recruits of 3 REI (3e Regiment Etranger d'Infanterie – 3rd Legion Infantry Regiment) march through Saigon in February 1947. They were one of the first units to engage in what proved to be a bitter and protracted struggle with the Viet Minh.

'Rapid Penetration' to dominate the countryside.

This strategy called for the use of vehicles to transport the men around. Reliance had to be placed upon a multitude of vehicles handed over by the Americans and the British, since the French automotive industry was in no position to provide all that were required. The same constraints applied to weapons and uniforms, with a mixture of American and British equipment being employed while French industry began the long process of introducing indigenous designs.

New Legion units evolved to meet the demands of this form of warfare, with 1 REC adopting amphibious vehicles for movement in flooded paddy fields, while two recently formed parachute battalions, *1er* and *2e Battalion Etranger de Parachutistes* (1st and 2nd Legion Parachute Battalion; 1 BEP and 2 BEP), were deployed to Indo-China as useful light infantry, ideal for rapid mobility operations (not least because they could be deployed by air if the need arose). By 1950, the French were facing 20,000 well-armed Viet Minh guerrillas under the command of

General Vo Nguyen Giap. Giap was given the opportunity to test his force in September 1950, when the French decided that Route Coloniale 4 (Colonial Route 4, a major communication route near that Chinese border) was too

Opposite: Legionnaires man a blockhouse somewhere in Indo-China. The French made great use of such positions in an attempt to control the countryside and reduce movement by the Viet Minh. Such positions were often attacked, and the relatively flimsy construction of many of the blockhouses made them vulnerable to enemy shellfire.

Above: Legion paratroops take a cigarette break near Hanoi while awaiting transport. The group includes two Germans, a Frenchman, an Italian and a Yugoslavian. They are armed with a mixture of weapons, the most obvious of which is the folding-stocked M2 Carbine carried across the chest of the man standing at back left.

dangerous to hold. This led to orders to evacuate all garrisons from Cao Bang to Lang Son, giving the Viet Minh the chance to attack the French as they withdrew.

Cao Bang and Dong Khe

The French appreciated that the most difficult part of the withdrawal would be the evacuation of Cao Bang, held by elements of 3 REI and a battalion of Moroccan troops under Colonel Charton. It was decided that they would be assisted

by *Groupement Bayard*, a column made up of another two battalions of Moroccans and 1 BEP. The plan was made more complicated when Giap launched an attack against the outpost at Dong Khe, held by 2nd Battalion of 3 REI. Just after midnight on 19 September 1950, the legionnaires found themselves under heavy fire. The Viet Minh massed for an assault, which went in at around 10:00 the next morning. Fighting continued until dawn on 20 September, with the

legionnaires fighting against near-impossible odds. Eighty-five legionnaires were killed and another 140 captured out of a garrison of 230. The five survivors broke through enemy lines to report the disaster. Although Giap had lost 800 men in the attack, he was now in control of RC 4, and had isolated Cao Bang.

In response, the combined Moroccan/Legion parachute column was ordered to retake Dong Khe, a ridiculous instruction given

Above: Legionnaires using amphibious armoured vehicles advance across the marshland to the south of Saigon as they carry out operations against the Viet Minh during November 1950. The French armed forces were still equipped with an almost bewildering array of French, American and British equipment at this point, and it would be some time before standardization upon French-made items took place.

Above: Legionnaires in action in a Vietnamese paddy-field during the fighting in 1950. The man in the foreground is armed with an M1924/29 light machine gun, an effective and robust weapon that was well-liked for its ability to deliver automatic fire.

the strength of the enemy forces confronting the column. Nevertheless, the column commander, Colonel Lepage, did as he was told and marched on Dong Khe. He split his force into two smaller columns, only to find that a huge Viet Minh force was waiting for them.

An attack in strength by the Viet Minh drove *Groupement Bayard* off RC 4 and into the jungle. The 1 BEP was given the task of protecting the rear of the column as it retreated, and suffered heavy

casualties as it sought to break contact with the pursuing Viet Minh. They eventually succeeded, and found Lepage's force in the Coc Xa gorge.

Now 1 BEP was at the top of the gorge, and thus above *Groupement Bayard*. The paratroopers had to fight their way down the slopes of the gorge to rejoin their colleagues, which required them to force a way through the Viet Minh. While they succeeded, they lost over 100 killed.

Rescue Mission

The column from Cao Bang was now given orders to go to the aid of *Groupement Bayard*, the irony of having to go to the assistance of their would-be rescuers not being lost on Charton and the men of 3 REI. They destroyed all their transport and set off into the jungle on foot. By 6 October, the Cao Bang column had reached Coc Xa, only to find that the area was swarming with Viet Minh troops who were in the process of trying to destroy the remnants of *Groupement Bayard*.

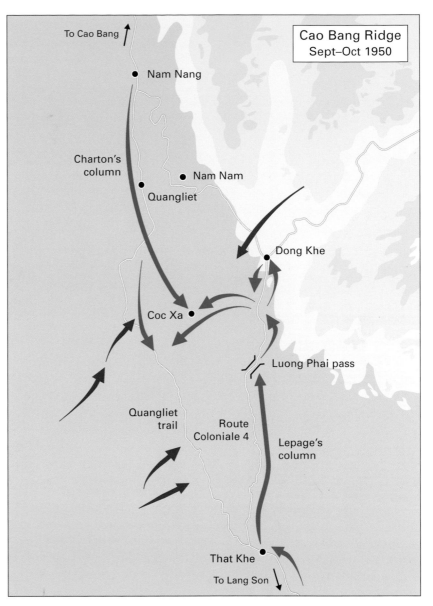

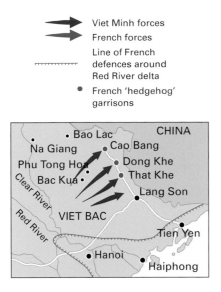

Above: The battle of the Cao Bang Ridge took place in the context of determined efforts by the French to maintain their position along the Chinese border. Ultimately, the French high command decided that the garrisons were too exposed, and should be withdrawn.

Right: The evacuation of French forces along Route Coloniale 4 proved to be a disaster as the Viet Minh put in heavy attacks against the force sent to assist those withdrawing from Cao Bang. Although the column from Cao Bang met up with the relief column, the two forces were decimated in a rear-guard action, notable for the sacrifice made by the Legion's paratroopers as they tried to break out into the jungle.

Charton's column arrived in the midst of the combat, and found access to the gorge barred by the Viet Minh. The ensuing fighting was incredibly fierce, and as the Viet Minh gained the upper hand, the Moroccan troops of Lepage's force panicked. This spread rapidly to Charton's Moroccan troops, and a rout ensued as the legionaries tried desperately to fight off the Viet Minh while the majority of the Moroccans fled into the jungle. By dawn on 7 October, there were only 450 legionnaires left, facing around 9000 Viet Minh. The situation was clearly hopeless, but the legionnaires from 1 BEP and 2nd Battalion 3 REI were determined to break out, and launched a vigorous assault. Incredibly, the survivors of 1 BEP managed to smash through Viet Minh lines after several hours, and struck out for friendly territory. Charton, meanwhile, ordered his men to split into small groups and make for Lang Son.

The survivors fought on through the jungle, but only 23 avoided death or capture – both Lepage and

Above: Legion paratroopers seen shortly after landing at Dien Bien Phu. The hilly terrain around the Legion base can be clearly seen, and the Viet Minh's control of the hill line meant that they were able to subject the legionnaires to heavy artillery bombardment throughout the battle.

Charton were taken prisoner. The battle along the Cao Bang ridge cost the French over 4000 men; 1 BEP and 3rd Battalion of 3 REI ceased to exist, while the casualties sustained by 2nd Battalion 3 REI were heavy enough to render the unit temporarily ineffective. The Viet Minh were encouraged by their success, and launched several attacks in 1951, all of which foundered when they ran into the Legion – 5 REI defeated the Viet Minh at Mao Khe; 13 DBLE beat off an attack on the Day River, while in October, 2 BEP crushed the insur-

gents at the battle of Nghia Lo. A similar pattern followed in 1952, when Giap sought to take the 'High Region' of Tonkin. Initial success encouraged Giap to attack an isolated base at Na San, which was occupied by 3 REI. After three days hard fighting, the Viet Minh attack was shattered.

Na San was representative of developing French strategy, which would have been quite familiar to a nineteenth-century legionnaire – namely the idea of establishing a base in territory that the enemy had previously dominated, and using it

as a hub for operations which would deny freedom of movement to the opponent.

While the principle worked at Na San, it was not applicable in all circumstances, as the French were to discover at Dien Bien Phu.

Dien Bien Phu

Dien Bien Phu was evacuated by the French in November 1952, but it was appreciated that this left the Viet Minh in control of the border with Laos. Consequently, it was decided that Dien Bien Phu must be retaken. The principles of establish-

Above: Lieutenant Boissy of 1st Battalion 2 REI stares wearily from his dugout, the extent of his wounds obvious. His tired yet determined demeanour epitomises the Legion's actions at Dien Bien Phu, where the legionnaires fought against massive odds with a vigour that surprised their opponents.

ing strongpoints – known as 'fortified hedgehogs' – seemed to work at Na San and elsewhere, and this prompted the recently arrived French commander-in-chief, General Henri Navarre, to agree to the establishment of a position at Dien Bien Phu making use of the fortified hedgehog principle. On 20 November 1953, men of the re-constituted 1 BEP were dropped into Dien Bien Phu to establish the foundations for the base. They were joined by another four Legion battalions (one each from 2 and 3 REI and two from 13 DBLE), and then another from 3 REI.

A perimeter was established around Dien Bien Phu airfield with six strongpoints dotted along it and another four outposts beyond. Nine of these positions were known by female names, allegedly after the mistresses of the garrison commander, the dashing cavalry officer Colonel Christian de Castries (the tenth strongpoint was called 'Sparrowhawk').

The theory behind the base at Dien Bien Phu seemed sensible – although deep in enemy territory, it could be resupplied from the air. Unfortunately, this assumed that the Viet Minh would be unable to place guns on the hills overlooking the Dien Bien Phu valley, a serious error of judgement that led to disaster. General Giap saw the opportunity to inflict a serious

Right: Legionnaires launch a counter-attack against Viet Minh positions at Dien Bien Phu, accompanied by an M24 Chaffee light tank. The American-designed Chaffee was an ideal vehicle for this sort of fighting, not least because of the potent effect of its 75mm (3in) gun against enemy strongpoints.

Above: Legionnaires bring in a dead body, most likely that of a comrade killed by the Viet Minh. The legionnaires were loathe to leave behind any of their comrades, dead or wounded, preferring to ensure that they were cared for (or buried) within the Legion 'family'.

reverse on the French, a prospect made more attractive by the fact that the base was held by a force heavily dependent upon the Legion for its manpower – defeating an elite French unit at Cao Bang had caused political uproar in France, and doing the same at Dien Bien Phu could undermine the will of the French to stay in Indo-China.

On the afternoon of 13 March 1954, the Viet Minh attacked Dien Bien Phu with a force about 50,000 strong. In addition to the infantry, Giap had assembled a regiment of artillery that had been manhandled up the slopes of the hills to give a commanding field of fire over all the French positions.

At 17:00 on 13 March, artillery fire began falling upon the strongpoint named 'Beatrice' that was held by 13 DBLE. The opening salvo killed 13 DBLE's commanding officer, Major Roger Pegot, and the second strongpoint commander, Colonel Jules Gaucher.

The barrage was followed by a human-wave assault by the Viet Minh, and despite desperate resistance 13 DBLE was forced to fall back in the early hours of 14 March. Strongpoint 'Gabrielle' fell to similar tactics the next day.

The battle continued with Viet Minh bombardments of the defences and the airstrip upon which the base depended for resupply. The French artillery commander, the one-armed Colonel Charles Piroth, appreciated that the Viet Minh, by taking control of the hills, could now bombard Dien Bien Phu at will, and blamed himself for not destroying the enemy guns.

In despair, he retired to his dug-out, and unable to cock a semi-automatic pistol with just one hand, pulled a pin from a hand grenade and let it fall to the ground. He died instantly in the ensuing blast.

Right: The bold decision to create a stronghold deep in Viet Minh territory came to fruition at Dien Bien Phu. The Legion found itself holding a position that was extremely difficult to defend, using a system of fortification to protect the town's airstrip, thus enabling resupply to take place. Plans to use the base to push into Viet Minh territory to engage the guerrillas did not go to plan as the Viet Minh invested the Legion positions in an epic action.

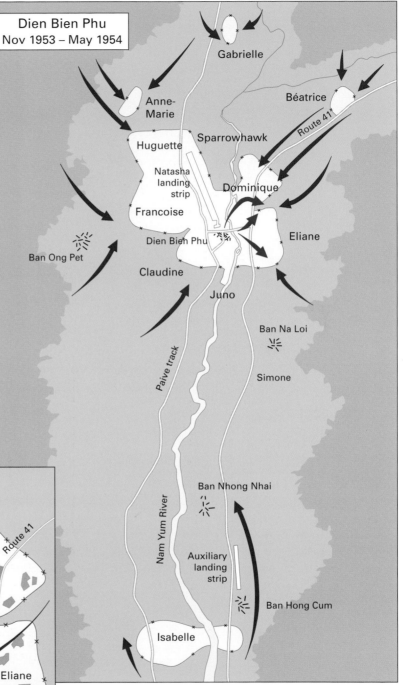

French strong points

Viet Minh assaults

French counterattacks

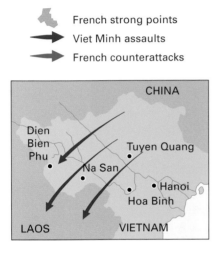

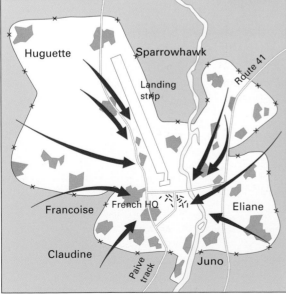

Left: The final assault against the remaining Legion positions took place on 3 May 1954. 'Huguette' and 'Claudine' were attacked first, and 'Eliane' fell on 6 May, leaving just 'Isabelle' and the French HQ. Finally, at 17:30 on 7 May 1954, the command post surrendered. The men at 'Isabelle' attempted a breakout, but only 12 men escaped.

Above: Legionnaires captured at Dien Bien Phu stream past the camera, heading for captivity. The Viet Minh proved harsh jailers, and a combination of wounds, disease and brutal treatment meant that only a very small percentage of those taken prisoner survived the ordeal of imprisonment.

Piroth's suicide perhaps epitomized the despair that would be associated with Dien Bien Phu. Although reinforcements were parachuted in along with supplies, the situation became progressively worse.

Lacking confidence in de Castries, the Legion officers staged a coup and politely informed the Colonel that he had been relieved of control over the battle, although he would remain nominally in command. De Castries, perhaps aware of the limitations of a cavalryman in positional warfare, accepted with little fuss.

Despair

The Viet Minh resumed their attacks, and the strongpoints 'Isabelle', 'Eliane' and 'Dominique' were next to be attacked. The legionnaires holding 'Isabelle' refused to retreat, but 'Dominique' and 'Eliane' fell, only to be retaken by a counter-attack launched by 2 REI. Nonetheless, the Viet Minh inexorably advanced. From 10 April, reinforcements arrived in an airdrop in the shape of 2 BEP, but the attrition in the fighting was such that there was a need for yet more manpower. This came in the form of volunteers from 3 and 5 REI, none of whom had ever made a parachute jump before, but who were prepared to take the risk of a single jump into Dien Bien Phu in an attempt to aid their comrades.

On 23 April, an attempt to retake strongpoint 'Hugette' failed with heavy casualties. By the end of the month, there were very few defenders left, and air supply efforts were being hampered by effective ground fire and the need to fly above the threat posed by the Viet Minh guns.

German Recruits – Myth and Reality

The Legion's relationship with Germany is one of some controversy, with many popular accounts suggesting that the Legion's forces in Indo-China after World War II contained an unhealthy number of former members of the *Waffen*-SS who sought continued employment in the military, seeing the Legion's willingness to grant anonymity as the ideal way of avoiding war crimes trials.

In fact, the truth was more complex. The Legion had always recruited a large number of German citizens. After World War II ended, Germany was utterly ruined, and many men sought an escape, with the Legion appearing an attractive option. This led to recruitment of a large number of Germans by the Legion, including ex-prisoners of war.

The end result was that up to 60 per cent of the Legion was of German origin during the Indo-China war. However, most of the recruits were not SS veterans, for the simple reason that the Legion deliberately excluded such men. Many of the Germans were, in fact, simply desperate young men trying to escape the privations of post-war Germany, and a large proportion (just over 40 per cent) were under the age of twenty-one. Rather than the brutal SS veterans so popularly believed to have fought in Indo-China, the Legion drew upon a mix of former soldiers from regular units and raw youngsters.

Consequently the airdrops were less than accurate, and supplies fell outside the contracting perimeter straight into the hands of the enemy. By 6 May, only 'Isabelle' was still under French control. Suggestions from the French high command in Hanoi that a breakout should be attempted were rejected. On 7 May, Dien Bien Phu surrendered. Over 4000 men, including 1500 legionnaires, had been killed in the defence, and 7000 were taken prisoner. Only 12 managed to evade capture and reach French lines, and they could regard themselves as fortunate, since most of the prisoners died in captivity.

The effect of the Viet Minh victory upon the French Government was immediate – it was defeated in parliament, and the new administration started the process of detaching itself from a colonial possession which was no longer tenable. The French negotiated a settlement at a summit in Geneva, and over 100 years of French rule in Indo-China came to an end.

Algeria

As well as the nationalist struggle in Indo-China, the French had to confront a problem much nearer to home in the form of a war launched in Algeria by nationalists seeking 'liberation' from French rule. Algeria was much more important to the French psyche than even Indo-China, since it was regarded as being an integral part of France rather than as an overseas colony.

Above: Legionnaires on watch in the oppressive heat of the Algerian desert. The success of operations in the desert forced the FLN into the cities, where it was able to conduct a wide-ranging guerrilla campaign against European civilians and Algerians loyal to the French.

The Algerian independence movement, through the auspices of the Algerian National Liberation Army (the ALN), began armed attacks on the French in November 1953. The war was to last for eight more years, and was in essence a succession of encounters between French troops (particularly from the Legion, which was fighting on 'home ground') and small armed bands of insurgents.

The French made use of helicopters to assist in the deployment of their manpower, and this tactic proved most effective. In the deserts, the Legion were remarkably successful, dominating the enemy. In conjunction with the fortification of the Algerian border, thus denying the ALN supplies, the French gained the upper hand. However, by driving the ALN out of the desert and into the cities, the French created more problems for themselves.

The Legion was employed to deny the ALN control of Algiers. The struggle, known as the battle of Algiers, was a resounding success

as the Legion defeated ALN cells in the city.

Torture and Terror

However, the robust methods employed in achieving this, accompanied by officially-sanctioned use of torture, lost support for the French amongst hitherto uncommitted Algerians. While the battle for Algiers may have been a military victory for the Legion, it was a strategic defeat for French efforts to win the war. The Legion carried out operations throughout Algeria, but as with Indo-China, the war became an increasingly divisive force in France. The Fourth Republic broke down, and Charles de Gaulle's arrival as president was perceived as being the only means by which the Algerian crisis could be resolved.

To the alarm of many in the French Army (and particularly the Legion), de Gaulle negotiated a French withdrawal and the granting of Algerian independence, rather than seeking to maintain some form of French presence. The consequences were serious. Members of the armed forces plotted to depose de Gaulle, and 1 REP was deeply involved in the coup attempt. When the plotters launched their effort in April 1961, they found that support was lacking. The coup failed, but many officers were arrested, and 1 REP was disbanded as a result of its involvement. An unexpected further consequence was the fact that the Legion had to leave the country that had been its home for a century. Questions were raised as to whether the formation should be disbanded, but the professionalism of the Legion and its value to France was such that this notion was swiftly abandoned.

Instead, the Legion moved to its new home at Aubagne, and reconfigured itself for operations in the post-colonial era, in which it was to become part of France's ability to respond rapidly to crises throughout the world.

Above: Legion paratroops enter the Belcourt district of Algiers on 24 January 1957. A wave of FLN attacks in this area led to reinforcement of the city as the battle was taken to the FLN in urban areas. Despite the very different conditions in the cities, the Legion was successful in suppressing FLN activity, although the robustness of their approach was to prove rather counter-productive.

The Modern Legion

The last decades of the twentieth century saw the Legion make numerous combat and peacekeeping deployments around the world. Its professional status ensures that it will remain at the heart of French military response options.

Algerian independence posed a major problem for the Legion, and not just because it required a new home. Serious questions were asked about whether the Legion should continue to exist – a 20,000-strong force that had been used as a means to control French colonies was left without an empire to defend. In addition, the politicization of certain elements of the Legion, leading to the attempted coup in 1961 by *1er Régiment Etranger de Parachutistes* (1st Legion Parachute Regiment; 1 REP), seemed to suggest that the force could not be trusted. As a counter to these arguments for disbanding the Legion, proponents of retaining the force pointed to the

Above: Admiring European settlers watch as legionnaires parade through Algiers to commemorate Bastille Day, 1956. Perhaps unsurprisingly, the settlers were very much against the idea of Algerian independence, and were a major source of support to the French forces in North Africa.

fact that it was a highly professional and battle-hardened formation, and that it would be ridiculous to lose so much experience. The final decision by de Gaulle's administration struck a balance between the two poles of the argument.

Army of Africa

As a part of the Army of Africa, there was no doubt that much of the Legion's work had disappeared along with Algeria. Between 1959 and 1964, 32 Army of Africa units were disbanded. The Legion escaped this fate, however. Instead of complete disbandment, major restructuring took place.

The Legion was reduced from 20,000 strong to an establishment of just 8000 soldiers; 1 REP (disgraced after its involvement in the coup attempt) and *2e Régiment Etranger de Cavalerie* (2nd Legion Cavalry Regiment; 2 REC) disappeared completely. The *4e Régiment Etranger d'Infanterie* (4th Legion Infantry Regiment; 4 REI) was sent to French Sahara to assist with work at the French nuclear test site, then it was disbanded as a fighting regiment. It was reconstituted as the Legion's headquarters unit at Castelnaudary in 1977.

Also disbanded was 5 REI, and its lineage passed to a unit based on Tahiti. This unit was known variously as 5 RE, 5 REI and 5 RMP (Régiment Mixte du Pacifique), with the latter becoming the more familiar term, since the regiment employed both Legion and other army personnel, particularly engineers. In later years, the fact that 5 RMP had a Legion heritage could easily be overlooked. This unit finally disbanded in 2000 as French

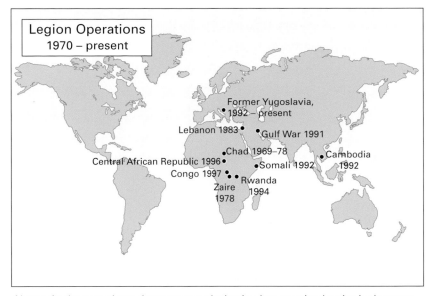

Above: As the map above demonstrates, the Legion has remained active in the years since French colonial operations came to a close. The deployments to Chad marked the longest-standing commitment, but a series of peacekeeping operations and humanitarian interventions have kept the Legion extremely busy, either with short, sharp actions, such as that at Kolwezi, or involvement in the delivery of aid.

forces reduced their presence in French Polynesia. As part of a bilateral agreement between France and the newly independent Algeria, 1 REC and 2 REP were allowed to stay in Algeria, but this only allowed for a French presence for five years.

It was not until 1966 that the Legion's basic training and administrative centre at Aubagne was established, and a year after this 1 REC moved to France. This was the first time that a Legion unit had been based permanently on the French mainland since the regiment had been formed 136 years earlier. For its first task on French soil, 1 REC used its armoured vehicles to guard the French nuclear deterrent bases. Meanwhile, 2 REP was sent to set up a new base at Calvi on Corsica. The French Government now sought to main-

tain influence around the world by sending troops into trouble spots as appropriate. This political strategy led to the creation of the Rapid Action Force, a rapid-deployment unit that preceded the much-heralded American Rapid Deployment Force (later Central Command or CENTCOM).

The 2 REP also underwent a change in focus – having been simply airborne infantry up until the late 1960s, they reorganized so that each company had a specific specialization, making the unit a much more versatile force than previously.

As 2 REP was in the process of developing its new skills, it found itself being deployed to the former French colony of Chad. The deployment marked the start of three decades of Legion involvement with the troubled country.

The Legion and Post-Colonial Africa

Although France withdrew from Algeria, Tunisia and Morocco in the 1960s, it has remained a constant presence on the African continent, often in the form of the Legion. Successive French governments have perceived Africa as being of strategic importance to France, as well as feeling some moral responsibility to many of the nations that were once ruled from Paris. As a result, the French rapid reaction forces were created to intervene in the region should military assistance be requested. This led to deployments in Chad, Rwanda, Djibouti, Zaire and the Cote d'Ivore amongst others as French forces were required to undertake a variety of tasks ranging from training through to hostage rescue. The versatility of the Legion and its ability to deploy quickly has proved to be of critical importance to French involvement in Africa. The most obvious deployment in the 1970s and 1980s was to Chad to try to maintain some stability in the country. Although this was not an easy task, some commentators credit French intervention with saving the state from complete collapse in the same manner in which Somalia later imploded, with a massive humanitarian crisis following the breakdown of the state and its functions.

Chad

Chad gained independence from France in 1960, but remained closely linked to the former colonial power. It joined the Central African Republic, Congo and Gabon as part of a multilateral military assistance pact with Paris. The pact gave the French the use of a base outside the Chadian capital N'Djamena (called Fort-Lamy in 1960), as well as granting the French the automatic right to overfly the country. France, in return for these rights, was to provide each nation with defence from external threats and was to help maintain internal security if requested.

The security clause meant that each signatory of the pact could request French intervention to maintain the security of its government. The French Government, however, reserved the right to treat each request on a case-by-case basis, thus opening the possibility of a refusal if involvement would be contrary to French national interest as perceived by the government. The Chadian Government also signed a military technical assistance agreement under which the French provided equipment, training and advisers. N'Djamena thus took on the function of providing one of the main French bases in Africa, giving France a facility for the rapid deployment of troops to any of the former French African colonies that required protection.

It was not long before Chad called for help. Chad was split on distinct tribal and religious lines, with those in the north being Islamic Arab and Berber tribes, while in the south black African Christian and animist tribes predominated. The tensions between the two communities rose until conflict was inevitable. A rebellion against President Tombalbaye's government broke out in 1965. The rebels formed themselves into the Front for the National Liberation of Chad (FROLINAT), and it soon became clear that the Chadian Government could not contain the violence.

As a result, a request for assistance was delivered to Paris, and from April 1969 troops were sent to help contain the rebellion. The Legion was deployed as part of the package. They found that the traditional problems associated with fighting in the desert remained, many of which would have been familiar to legionnaires at the end of the nineteenth century.

Disease, the difficulty in finding drinking water, logistical challenges and the doubtful support of some of the local population were familiar foes. The intervention mainly comprised patrol operations, although there were one or two notable actions where the Legion was involved. In October 1969, a French aircraft spotted a small group of armed men resting in the bush, and a Legion column was sent to investigate. It transpired that the men were part of a group of 100 rebels. A brisk battle ensued, and 68 of the enemy were killed.

Anti-insurgency Actions

The following year, a company of legionnaires was sent to seize the airstrip at Zouar, which was under rebel control. The rebels were taken completely by surprise by an airborne landing by 2 REP, and they retreated to their hideouts in the nearby hills. The paratroops followed them, and engaged them. The ensuing battle lasted for a day and a half, and by the end of it, the

Above: A legionnaire armed with a MAT-49 submachine gun stands guard over Chadian youths rounded up after a skirmish between the Legion and local rebels sometime during the French deployment in 1978.

enemy force had been routed. Some 50 rebels were killed, for the loss of one dead legionnaire. A few months later, in November 1970, another battle between 2 REP and a concentrated enemy force left another 50 rebels dead.

As well as acting against the rebels, the Legion was employed in training Chadian forces so that they would be better able to deal with the revolt. By 1972, it was felt that the rebellion had been suppressed sufficiently to allow the French force to be reduced. This did not, however, mean the end of the fight-ing. Libya (supporting the northern tribes) occupied the mineral-rich Aouzou Strip that lay between it and Chad in 1973, and began pro-viding support to the rebels.

Tombalbaye was overthrown in 1975, and disagreements between the French and General Felix Malloum's government resulted in the removal of the few remaining French combat forces. Despite this, the French remained committed to the original pact, which was to see French forces return to Chad in 1978, when the political situation deteriorated.

An armoured squadron from 1 REC and a company from 1 REI were sent, and began a series of short operational tours for the Legion. The tours were short because of the experiences of the 1969 deployment, which had seen men fall ill if they were in country for much longer than four months. Yet the Legion saw exposure to operations in Chad as offering immensely valuable experience to its soldiers.

The first action by the Legion came in April 1978 at the northern town of Salal, when an armoured

Above: An unconventionally dressed legionnaire – possibly operating as a mercenary – armed with an FN FAL rifle rather than a standard French weapon. The picture was taken in Zaire in the 1980s, and the FAL was one of the weapons of that nation's army. In the 1970s, legionnaires also made some use of the FAL in preference to the MAS-49, since the former had a larger magazine capacity and the ability to fire on full-automatic.

car from a 1 REC patrol engaged a rebel armoured personnel carrier and destroyed it. The rebel troops in the town were persuaded to leave by a swift bombardment from the 1 REC patrol's 90mm (3.5in) guns. A month later, a combined 1 REC and 2 REP force took the town of Ati from the rebels before moving on to seize the neighbouring town of Djedda. The intervention ended in 1980, when General Malloum went into exile, and was replaced by General Goukouni Weddeye, the leader of one of the northern factions. The last elements of the Legion force left Chad in May 1980, the country apparently becoming more stable.

More political unrest ensued, however, with Goukouni being replaced by Hissen Habré. Habré had been prime minister under Malloum, and then an ally of Goukouni until the two disagreed, leading to renewed fighting. Libya intervened at Goukouni's request, only for Colonel Qadhafi to withdraw his troops when the French Government complained. Habré finally managed to drive Goukouni into the north of Chad, beginning the so-called Second Republic. Although in control of the capital, Habré did not hold all of the country, which was, in effect, partitioned along the 16th parallel. A Libyan military presence remained in the north, especially in the Aouzou Strip.

Libyan Incursions

A renewed offensive in 1983 by Goukouni's GUNT faction (supported by the Libyans), prompted Habré to make an urgent request for direct intervention. President Mitterand was reluctant to accede to the plea, but after appeals from other francophone African states and from Washington (now concerned about Libyan intentions) the French launched Operation Manta. The French forces acted as a buffer between the GUNT/Libyan forces and the Chadian Government troops, and a peace settlement was negotiated during 1984. Both France and Libya were to withdraw their troops, while some legitimacy was granted to Goukouni, who was allowed to establish a provisional government for the territory under his control. The Libyans broke their part of the agreement, and in February 1986 pushed into Chadian

territory. The Libyan incursion triggered a further French deployment, Operation *Epervier*. The Legion was committed along with French air assets, but solely for defensive purposes. The French Government wished to send a clear signal to the Libyans, however, to convince them that French forces would fight if the Libyans pushed south of the 16th Parallel.

To achieve this, an air raid was launched against the newly built Ouadi Doum air base, which had been built in Goukouni-controlled territory by the Libyans. The attack succeeded in rendering the airfield temporarily unusable. Meanwhile,

an airlift of equipment to the Chadian Government took place. The situation appeared to have stabilized, but the GUNT faction then broke apart as the Libyans attempted to increase their level of control over the north of the country.

The Libyans now found themselves facing a rebellion in which Goukouni asked Habré for assistance as nationalism took precedence over internal dispute.

The Libyans reacted vigorously, moving several thousand troops into northern Chad. The Chadian Government then launched an offensive into the north, which met

Above: Legionnaires survey the streets of Mogadishu late in 1992 while participating in Operation Restore Hope, the United Nations'
effort to alleviate the humanitarian crisis stemming from the Somali civil war. Armed peacekeepers were required to try to prevent
the warring factions from seizing food aid and using it as a means of controlling the starving local population.

Legion Ceremonies

The Legion has a number of ceremonial days, but the two most important are Camerone Day, commemorated every year on 30 April, and Bastille Day. Camerone was first celebrated on 16 February 1906, rather than on the actual anniversary of the battle. The reason for this was that the commemoration was part of the ceremonies that occurred when 1 RE received the *Legion d'Honneur* in recognition of its services. In the aftermath of the ceremony, it was felt that the commemoration of Camerone should be repeated. This was duly done, with the ceremony being moved to the true anniversary of the battle. The commemoration took on greater significance after World War I, when it was used as a means of illustrating the history and tradition of the unit.

In 1931, General Paul Rollet decided that the commemoration should be made more formal, serving as a remembrance of all those who had died while on Legion service. On 30 April 1931, a parade was held at Sidi-bel-Abbès, Algeria, attended by dignitaries from France and allied nations, and this established the pattern for future years. The ceremony began with a march-past, a recitation of an account of the battle and the parading of the wooden hand of Captain Jean Danjou as the Legion band played 'Le Boudin'. This format is followed today at Castelnaudary, while Legion units based elsewhere also hold some form of commemoration of the day.

Bastille Day, on 14 July each year, was not something the Legion participated in for many years. However, in 1939, the first Legion involvement occurred, and the Legion is now just as much a part of the celebrations as any other military unit. The Legion's parade is led by its pioneers (pictured below), recognizable as the only men in the Legion allowed to sport beards, and carrying ceremonial axes rather than rifles.

with considerable success. Qadhafi responded by ordering air strikes well to the south of the 16th parallel, and this prompted another French attack on Ouadi Doum, as well as the deployment of more troops to support Operation *Epervier*, including elements of 2 REI.

By late 1987, both sides were exhausted, and the Libyans had been evicted from all of northern Chad apart from the Aouzou Strip. Negotiations over the Strip continued against a background of internal political strife in Chad, until finally, in 1994, the International Court of Justice ordered that the Strip be returned to Chad. In amongst this upheaval, the Legion maintained a presence in Chad as a nominal peacekeeping force. The legionnaires carried out a variety of activities, mostly relating to training, but also provided basic medical care for tribesmen. By the late-1990s, the challenge presented by Chad had effectively ended.

Kolwezi

The Legion found itself called upon to carry out an urgent rescue mission in May 1978, at the town of Kolwezi, in Zaire (now the Democratic Republic of Congo). Early in May 1978, 3000 Katangese rebels crossed into Zaire from Angola, and headed for Kolwezi. Their objective was to besiege the town, a major mining centre, and in so doing destabilize Zaire by attacking one of the major elements of the national economy.

The rebels, members of the Cuban-sponsored Congo National Liberation Front (FNLC), broke into the town centre and massacred scores of locals. Much of Kolwezi's

Above: Members of 2 REP chat with Zairian paratroops prior to the attack on Kolwezi in 1978. The aircraft in the background is a Transall C.160, the standard para-dropping aircraft used by 2 REP.

mining operation involved European specialists, and the FNLC threatened them, hoping to embarrass the Zairean government.

The Zairean army was sent to deal with the rebels, but was routed, and an attempt by Zaire's parachute unit, their army's elite force, met with disaster – many of the paratroopers were killed while still in their parachutes, with the rebels bayoneting some as they landed. As a result, the Zairean leadership asked France for military assistance. President Giscard d'Estaing gave orders for 2 REP to carry out a rescue operation. Under the command of Colonel Phillipe Erulin, 2 REP headed for Zaire, arriving there on 17 May 1978. Confusion then reigned, since a variety of orders and counterorders reached the legionnaires, who also discovered that they would be dropped into Kolwezi by Zairean aircraft.

This was not a problem, since the Zaireans used the C-130 and Transall C.160, the same aircraft that 2 REP were used to jumping from. However, the Zaireans were also providing the parachutes in the form of the American T-10 pattern 'chute. While they waited for some operational clarity, the legionnaires familiarized themselves with the recently provided parachutes. The presence of the media also posed problems, and it soon became clear that the FNLC would be made aware of the fact that the Legion was being sent to resolve the situation in Kolwezi. Concerned that this might prompt a massacre of the hostages, Erulin brought the mission forward.

The new timetable had important implications, since the Zairean air

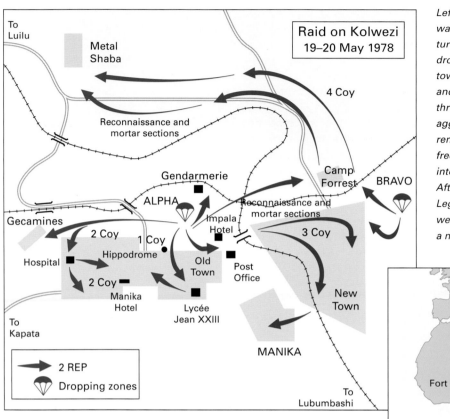

Raid on Kolwezi
19–20 May 1978

To Luilu

Metal Shaba

4 Coy

Reconnaissance and mortar sections

Gendarmerie

ALPHA

Camp Forrest

BRAVO

Reconnaissance and mortar sections

Gecamines

Impala Hotel

2 Coy

1 Coy

3 Coy

Hospital

Hippodrome

Old Town

Post Office

2 Coy

New Town

Manika Hotel

Lycée Jean XXIII

To Kapata

MANIKA

2 REP

Dropping zones

To Lubumbashi

Left: The parachute assault on Kolwezi was a particularly risky venture, but turned into a brilliant success. Using two drop zones, 2 REP moved through the town, driving the Katangan rebels out, and swiftly took control. The initial move through the town was followed by aggressive patrolling in which the remaining rebels were denied the freedom of movement to either escape into the bush or to return to the town. After 48 hours, Kolwezi was firmly under Legion control, and the trapped civilians were finally freed from the threat of a massacre.

CORSICA
Calvi

CHAD

Fort Lamy

ZAIRE

Kinshasa

Kamina
Kolwezi
Lubumbashi

ANGOLA

ZAMBIA

force proved unable to deliver the lift capacity it had promised. Instead of the seven aircraft that were needed to drop 2 REP, only five – four C-130s and a single Transall – appeared. Erulin decided to press on.

Into Action

On the morning of 19 May, the paratroopers (minus 4th Company who could not be accommodated on the available aircraft), set out for Kolwezi. The aircraft were packed, and Erulin later remarked that even the most hardened parachutists were alarmed at the cramped conditions. The flight from the airbase at Kinshasa to Kolwezi lasted five hours, and the men of 2 REP reached the drop-zone at 15:40.

The jump took the rebels by surprise, but the legionnaires were leaving nothing to chance. They regrouped quickly, and pushed on towards their objectives. The 1st Company was to take the local school; 2nd Company the hospital and the offices of the mining company; 3rd Company would seize the Impala hotel and the Post Office. As the legionnaires moved towards the town, the rebels did not offer a great deal of resistance, but as the troops reached the outskirts the rebels started to fight back. However, the rebel forces proved little match for the legionnaires, who were moving forward in ruthless fashion. Those rebels who

chose to stand and fight stood little chance. The legionnaires killed over 100 rebels as they moved towards their objectives, and were in control of the town just two hours after landing.

The second wave of paratroops, from 4th Company, arrived the next morning, and their sniper teams proved particularly useful in engaging the rebels, inflicting more casualties. Soldiers of 2 REP conducted aggressive patrolling, aimed at killing or capturing any rebels who were found. In the middle of the afternoon 4th Company ran into stiff resistance, and promptly called in Support Company, who set about mortaring the rebels. At this point, a column of lorries carrying more rebel soldiers appeared, supported by two light tanks. Support Company destroyed the tanks with 89mm (3.5in) anti-tank rockets, and a mixture of mortars, machine guns and rifle fire raked the column. Within a matter of minutes, the entire enemy column was ablaze, with the survivors fleeing for the bush. Now in control of Kolwezi, 2 REP moved forward to carry out mopping-up operations. Some of

the rebels tried to resist, but this did not achieve much beyond briefly delaying the legionnaires as they advanced.

The last fighting took place on 25 May when a Katangan force was wiped out as it attempted to reach safety over the Angolan border. With little else to do, the legionnaires were withdrawn, and 2 REP flew back to Corsica on 5 June. Although the rebels succeeded in killing scores of the inhabitants of Kolwezi, the arrival of the Legion saved hundreds more, and demonstrated the shock effect that could be achieved by rapid use of a

versatile, self-contained force of paratroopers.

Peacekeeping: Lebanon

The Israeli invasion of Lebanon in 1982 left a situation in which the Palestine Liberation Organization (PLO) was left with the choice of fighting to the death, with the associated risk to the inhabitants of Beirut, or of evacuating the city. A deal was agreed in which the PLO would leave Lebanon and go to nearby Arab nations that were willing to accommodate the fighters. To oversee this arrangement, a multi-national force was deployed,

Above: Legionnaires stand guard over the coffins containing the bodies of the five legionnaires killed in the rescue operations at Kolwezi. The dead legionnaires were awarded posthumous decorations and buried with full military honours.

Above: A legionnaire looks on as a medical worker tends to two wounded children in Chad in 1983. The Legion have played a notable part in peacekeeping operations in Central Africa throughout the last 30 years.

with 2 REP being given the task of monitoring the departure of the Palestinians.

Arriving on 20 August, the legionnaires patrolled the port area to ensure that the PLO members left unmolested. The PLO leader, Yasser Arafat, was due to depart on 30 August, but intelligence information suggested that he might be in danger of being assassinated.

As a result, the *Commandos de Recherche et d'Action dans la Profondeur* (CRAP) element of 2 REP was tasked with escorting Arafat, a duty they carried out with little fuss. The legionnaires then moved to take over the so-called 'Green Line' that divided Beirut. The legionnaires then set about serving as part of the French contribution to the multi-national peace-

keeping force, and 2 REP went home to Calvi in September.

The Legion returned to Lebanon in May 1983, when 2 REI and 1 REC participated in the rotation of French forces. Both carried out patrols through Beirut, meeting increasing hostility from local militia groups, who resented the fact that the peacekeepers were interfering with their efforts at

---

French Peacekeeping Forces in Lebanon 1982–84
Units and Commanders

11th Airborne Division
  (August–September 1982)
(Brigadier General Jacques Granger)
– 9th Marine Infantry Division
– 2nd Foreign Legion Parachute Regiment
– 3rd Marine Airborne Battalion
– 9th Headquarters Support Battalion
– 17th Airborne Engineers Battalion

11th Airborne Division
  (September 1982–January 1983)
(Brigadier General Jacques Granger)
– 8th Marine Airborne Battalion
– 1st Airborne Hussars Battalion
– 2nd Marine Infantry Battalion
– 17th Airborne Engineers Battalion
– 1st Headquarters Support Battalion

9th Marine Infantry Division
  (January–May 1983)
(Brigadier General Michel Datin)
– 9th Marine Infantry Battalion
– 3rd Marine Infantry Battalion
– 11th Marine Artillery Battalion
– Marine Armoured Infantry Battalion

31st Brigade (May–September 1983)
(Brigadier General Jean-Claude Coulon)
– 21st Marine Infantry Battalion
– Engineers Company,
  21st Marine Infantry Battalion

– 2nd Foreign Legion Infantry Regiment
– 1st Foreign Legion Cavalry Regiment
– 17th Airborne Engineers Battalion

11th Airborne Division
  (September 1983 – January 1984)
(Brigadier General Francois Cann)
– 3rd Marine Airborne Battalion
– 6th Airborne Infantry Battalion
– 6th Airborne Battalion (company)
– 1st Airborne Infantry Battalion (company)
– 9th Airborne Infantry Battalion (company)
– 1st Airborne Hussars Battalion (platoon)
– 17th Airborne Engineers Battalion (company)
– 12th Field Artillery Battalion (battery)
– 7th Headquarters Airborne Support Battalion
  (support detachment)

9th Marine Infantry Division
  (February–March 1984)
(Brigadier General Michel Datin)
– 9th Headquarters Support Battalion
  (detachment)
– 501st Tank Battalion (platoon)
– Marine Armored Infantry Battalion (platoon)
– Gendarmerie (MPs – platoon)
– 2nd Marine Infantry Battalion (2 companies)
– 12th Field Artillery Battalion (battery) – later
  replaced by 68th Field Artillery Battalion
– 59th Engineer Company
– 41st Transmission Battalion (company)

internecine conflict. The legionnaires carried out their task in trying circumstances, and were not sorry to leave.

Shortly after they had departed, 52 French soldiers were killed in a suicide bombing attack on French headquarters. On the same day, over 240 US Marines were killed in a similar attack, and this prompted the international community to take the decision that Lebanon could be left to its own devices. Withdrawal followed in 1984 – although the peacekeeping mission had been a failure, the Legion had done its job well, despite trying circumstances.

Rwanda

One of the less-glorious aspects of the international community's response to intra-state conflict occurred during the 1990s in Rwanda. Long-standing rivalry between the Tutsi and Hutu communities led to civil war in 1990. To protect French and Belgian nationals working in the country, 2 REP's 4th Company along with its CRAPs was sent to carry out an evacuation, under the auspices of Operation Noroît. After a 10-month stay in which their mere presence brought calm to the capital Kigali, they were replaced by 3rd Company. The mission went well, but worse was to befall Rwanda before long. In April 1994, President Habyarimana was killed when his aircraft was brought down as he returned from Burundi.

This incident was blamed on the Rwanda Patriotic Front (RPF), and members of the majority Hutu community started killing Tutsis, who were viewed as accomplices of the RPF. The genocide that ensued was

Above: A legionnaire shakes hands with a Zairean soldier as the two meet on the border between Zaire and Rwanda, 1994. The deployment of French troops was controversial, not least since it was alleged that the French government's instructions to the soldiers meant that the perpetrators of the genocide were allowed to continue their campaign with virtual impunity.

Above: A group of legionnaires cluster around an orphaned Rwandan child. The Legion found itself dealing with many orphans and bereaved amongst the tide of refugees trying to escape from the militias responsible for the wholesale killing of the Tutsis.

ignored by the international community, which appeared reluctant to intervene. Although it was clear that the killings amounted to genocide, many nations spoke of 'tribal killings', since recognizing that genocide was taking place would have made them liable to intervene according to the 1948 Genocide Convention.

Around one million people were killed and another million displaced within Rwanda. A further two million fled the country, many to Zaire (the exodus had a destabilizing effect on that country as well). Finally, in May 1994, the United Nations Security Council ratified

Resolution 918, aimed at strengthening the extant United Nations Assistance Mission for Rwanda (UNAMIR) with troops. There were no offers of assistance until France offered to intervene. The UN Security Council authorized French involvement on 22 June 1994 under Resolution 929. The Legion was chosen as part of the force that would carry out Operation *Turquoise*. Under this, the French established *Zones Humanitaires Sures* (ZHS), covering a fifth of Rwanda.

The creation of the ZHS was controversial, with some observers claiming that the French intended

to help the Hutu government by preventing total victory of the RPF. This meant that the rules of engagement for the peacekeeping force were biased towards the Hutus. The Hutus were not disarmed by the legionnaires, which also meant that the ZHS were less than safe. Those in the ZHS were given food and shelter, but they were not protected from the armed groups of extremist Hutus who continued to operate with impunity.

On 6 July 1994, the French Government signed a non-aggression pact with the RPF, and the French extricated the Legion over the next few months. Rwanda's

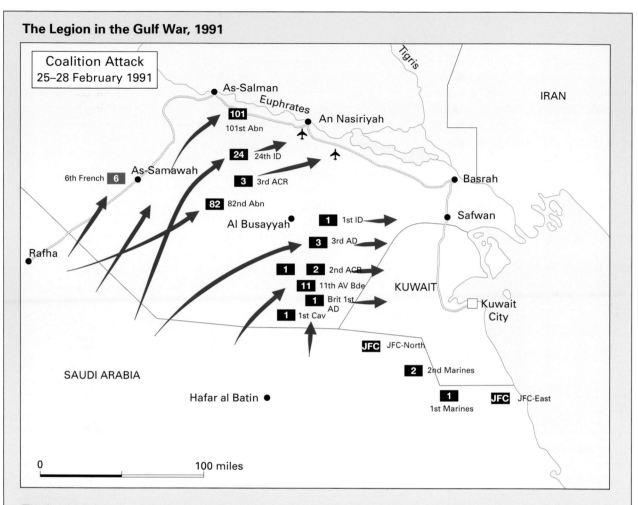

The Legion in the Gulf War, 1991

Coalition Attack
25–28 February 1991

IRAN

Tigris

As-Salman

Euphrates

An Nasiriyah

101 101st Abn

6th French **6**

As-Samawah

24 24th ID

3 3rd ACR

Basrah

82 82nd Abn

Al Busayyah

Safwan

1 1st ID

3 3rd AD

Rafha

1 **2** 2nd ACR

KUWAIT

11 11th AV Bde

1 Brit 1st AD

1 1st Cav

Kuwait City

JFC JFC-North

SAUDI ARABIA

2 2nd Marines

Hafar al Batin

1 1st Marines

JFC JFC-East

0   100 miles

The Legion's involvement in the war to liberate Kuwait from Iraqi occupation was marked by periods of confusion and frustration imposed by French politicians. France joined the American-led coalition sent to the region to remove Iraqi troops from Kuwait. Two Legion regiments, 2 REI and 2 REC, were part of the French force, but their participation looked as though it would be limited. Defence Minister Jean-Pierre Chevenement insisted that all decisions be approved by him. This risked making the planning process overly complex, so the other nations in the coalition simply continued planning without French input. As the United Nations deadline for Iraqi forces to leave Kuwait approached, the French Government decided that French forces, now under the title of the Daguet Division, would participate. The CRAP team from 2 REP arrived in the theatre on 12 February 1991 and began carrying out reconnaissance missions, along with an unsuccessful attack on the airfield at As-Salman; two men were killed and another 25 injured. After an air offensive of six weeks, Coalition ground units attacked on 24 February, and 2 REI led the way for the Daguet Division. The rest of Daguet rolled forward and took As-Salman on the Euphrates River in just 48 hours, with 2 REC and 2 REI leading the way. The war ended just 100 hours after the ground assault started, with the Legion's two units winning many accolades for their performance.

Above: The Legion's involvement in Operation Desert Storm was as part of the massive assault into Iraq, aimed at outflanking the troops occupying Kuwait.

recovery from the genocide is a slow process. The Legion deployment showed how difficult operations can be for even the most professional soldiers when political considerations limit their freedom of action. Similar frustrations were to be encountered in the Legion's other major peacekeeping operation in the Balkans.

The Balkans

The collapse of Yugoslavia in the early 1990s led to one of the most bitter civil wars of recent times.

Fighting spread from Croatia to Bosnia, and the UN authorized an international peacekeeping force for the region. The peacekeepers were to oversee a ceasefire and assist with the provision of humanitarian aid. Unfortunately, the peacekeepers, including elements of the Legion, found that their rules of engagement were too inflexible, and they could often do nothing to stop the killing of civilians.

In 1992, 2 REP was given the role of guarding the airport at Sarajevo, a task they carried out with their

usual robust approach. Snipers from all sides of the dispute proved a particular nuisance, not least since they were quite content to target civilians. The Legion set about carrying out counter-sniping missions, something that came as a most unpleasant surprise to the snipers, and settled down to the usual rotation of forces, with 2 REI replacing 2 REP in 1993.

The UN mandate remained less than effective, with the warring parties seemingly able to interfere with aid convoys at will and

Above: Legionnaires fan out as they patrol in Kosovo shortly after the arrival of the NATO peacekeeping force in 1999. The Legion's engineers played a notable part in assisting with local reconstruction projects as the Kosovar Albanians tried to rebuild their towns and villages in the aftermath of President Milosevic's ethnic cleansing campaign against them.

Above: French 120mm (4.9in) mortars on top of Mount Igman, Bosnia. When patience with the Bosnian Serbs finally ran out, mortar teams engaged a number of Serb targets as part of Operation Deliberate Force, a NATO campaign using air power and artillery to coerce the Bosnian Serbs into negotiating a peace settlement.

operate relatively unhindered by the presence of peacekeepers. As in Rwanda, 'safe havens' proved anything but, and civilians were massacred while UN troops proved unable to do anything to respond.

Eventually, in 1995, patience wore thin. The Bosnian Serbs, identified as the most recalcitrant of the warring groups, were subjected to Operation Deliberate Force. NATO bombing raids against key Serb targets helped to compel the Serbs to agree to the Dayton Peace Accords. The Accords were to be enforced by NATO rather than the UN, and 2 REP found itself involved in implementing the peace with a much more robust set of instructions. Once the peace terms had been implemented, peace-keepers remained in Bosnia.

The Legion continues to send units out to the former Yugoslavia. The legionnaires patrol the countryside, and carry out occasional raids in an effort to track down war criminals. Other operations include seizing weapons and explosives that remain left over from the war.

A similar pattern of operations confronts legionnaires in Kosovo, including escorting the Serbian minority in the province to and from church – the hatred between the Orthodox Serb and Muslim Kosovar Albanian communities remains strong, and the peacekeeping troops are frequently called upon to break up riots and keep the two communities apart.

The Legion Today and Tomorrow

The French Foreign Legion remains one of the most highly regarded military units in the world. Its reputation is hard won, and protected

Above: A legionnaire scans the perimeter of Sarajevo airport from the turret of his VAB armoured vehicle, looking out for anyone who might try to attack the RAF Hercules transport that can be seen landing in the background. The airport, which lay under Serbian guns, was the only means of getting aid into Sarajevo, and the UN forces made determined efforts to keep it open.

jealously by the legionnaires, for whom high standards remain important. As a professional, well-equipped and versatile force, the Legion is in the forefront of French military operations, being deployed rapidly to trouble-spots around the world. As well as retaining the key skills for fighting in conventional war, the Legion has increased its proficiency at peacekeeping, offering yet another capability to the French Government.

Such versatility means that the Legion will remain at the heart of French defence policy, giving it the opportunity to add to its legendary reputation in conflicts and crisis to come. Some of that reputation is based upon myth, misunderstanding and sometimes sheer fantasy, but even when this is stripped away, it is clear that the Legion remains a dedicated, proficient fighting formation, and amongst the world's elite.

Recruitment and Life in the Legion

Despite its world-wide fame, the Legion remains a rather mysterious outfit in the eyes of many. A number of myths and misconceptions have attached themselves to what the Legion is, what it does, and particularly to those who fill its ranks.

It is often assumed that the Legion is filled with a mixture of hardened criminals and romantics, all seeking to leave behind their previous lives, or to evade the law, or to lessen the pain of a broken heart. While this assumption may be true of some legionnaires, it is not helpful in trying to understand the men of the Foreign Legion. There is less misrepresentation when it comes to the training each legionnaire goes through. Legion training is indeed extremely tough, and in previous years was marked by terrifyingly strict discipline and brutal tests of endurance – some elements of which remain today.

However, the common image of the Legion only scratches the surface, and the men, their motives for joining and the training that they receive are all far more complex than popular perception would suggest. Most of the typical beliefs about the Legion are inaccurate, and do not give a true or full picture.

Joining the Legion

Joining the Legion is not as easy a task as may be supposed. The image of the unit as a home for misfits and criminals tends to lead to the assumption that almost anyone will be accepted. Such is far from the case. Despite – or perhaps because of – the reputed toughness of life as a legionnaire, there are far more recruits than are actually required. It is not uncommon for only 10 per cent of applicants to be accepted into the Legion, and in 1998, one recruiting centre turned away almost 45 per cent of those who sought to join.

While some potential legionnaires are rejected because of medical problems, others fail to be accepted for the surprising reason that they are married. The Legion takes the view that married individuals are unsuitable recruits – life in the Legion is hardly family-oriented, and the pay received by new recruits is inadequate to maintain a wife or family. Another obstacle to

Above: Legionnaires parading in full dress uniform. The white képis are notable, as are the shoulder boards, worn only for formal or ceremonial occasions. The Legion takes ceremony very seriously, and is highly regarded for its standard of drill.

joining the Legion attacks the stereotype of the typical legionnaire – having a criminal record may prove to be an instant barrier to acceptance. Whereas a 'no questions asked' attitude used to be common, the modern Legion can afford to be more selective in its choice, and invariably is.

The Legion is a true mixed-race force. While the officers of the Legion are overwhelmingly French (and those who have risen through the ranks of the Legion must adopt French citizenship before they can become an officer), the men – as the name of the unit suggests – are made up of a variety of nationalities. Despite the 'Foreign' in the title, however, a large proportion of recruits are French (although French nationals cannot officially serve as legionnaires), and explain away their French-sounding names and surprising fluency in the language by claiming to be from places such as Belgium or Switzerland.

All recruits will enter the Legion either by presenting themselves at a recruiting centre (there are over a dozen in France) or at a Gendarmerie, where they declare their intention of joining the Legion.

If the volunteer goes to a Gendarmerie, he will be collected by a junior non-commissioned officer (NCO) from the Legion and taken to a recruitment centre, where he will be relieved of his passport and other items. Money, clothes and personal possessions are taken from the recruit and placed into storage.

If the applicant is rejected, these items are returned to him upon departure; if the Legion decides to keep the recruit, his personal

Above: A poster outside a recruiting office, offering would-be recruits details of life in the Legion. It is debatable as to whether the Legion actually requires such posters, since the unit's reputation is such that it attracts a large number of men who have probably never even seen a recruitment poster.

effects will be sold and only his money (held on account) and passport will be handed back at the end of his service. He will see these items once more if successful in his efforts to join the Legion. The Legion, however, does not remove every personal item – watches, wallets (with a small amount of money) and washing and shaving gear are permitted, as is a bilingual dictionary. The latter is particularly useful, since those recruits who are unable to speak French must learn to do so, and very quickly. The applicant is issued with an army

The Legionnaire's Code of Honour

One of the tasks set for each would-be legionnaire is to learn the *Code d'honneur du Légionnaire* (Code of Honour of the Legionnaire). The recruit must be able to recite it in French, and from memory, so that it can be said at the ceremony at which the legionnaires receive the *képi blanc* for the first time.

1. *Legionnaire, tu es un volontaire servant la France ávec honneur et fidelite.*
2. *Chaque legionnaire est ton frere d'arme quelle que soit sa nationalite, sa race, sa religion. Tu lui manifestes toujours la solidarite etroitequi doit unir les membres d'une meme famille.*
3. *Respecteux des traditions, attache a tes chefs, la discipline et la camaradarie sont ta force, le courage et la loyaute tes vertus.*
4. *Fier de ton etat de legionnaire, tu le montres dans ta tenue toujours etegante, ton comportement toujours digne mais modeste, ton casernement toujours net.*
5. *Soldat d'elite, tu t'entrafnes avec rigueur, tu entretiens ton arme comme ton bien le plus precieux, tu as le souci constant de ta forme physique.*
6. *La mission est sacree, tu l'executes jusqu'au bout, a tout prix.*
7. *Au combat, tu agis sans passion et sans haine, tu respectes les ennemis vaincus, tu n'abandonnes jamais ni tes morts, ni tes blesses, ni tes armes.*

1. Legionnaire, you are a volunteer serving France with honour and fidelity.
2. Every legionnaire is your brother-in-arms regardless of his nationality, race, or religion. You will demonstrate this by the strict solidarity which must always unite members of the same family.
3. Respectful of traditions, devoted to your leaders, discipline and comradeship are your strengths, courage and loyalty your virtues.
4. Proud of your status as legionnaire, you display this in your uniform which is always impeccable, your behaviour always dignified but modest, your living quarters always clean.
5. An elite soldier, you will train rigorously, you will maintain your weapon as your most precious possession, you are constantly concerned with your physical form.
6. A mission is sacred, you will carry it out until the end, at all costs.
7. In combat, you will act without passion and without hate, you will respect the vanquished enemy, you will never abandon your dead or wounded, nor surrender your arms.

uniform and is set to work to keep him occupied. The work is usually menial in nature, and involves cleaning and/or helping in the kitchens. This labour is a useful introduction to the Legion, since for the junior ranks such chores – known as *corvée* – will be a part of daily life until they are promoted and thus excused the need to carry out these tasks.

At some point, the prospective recruit is relieved of his duties and will be subjected to a medical examination and an interview. As long as he has passed the medical, the recruit will have started the process that leads to his being presented with a contract to sign. Once the contract is signed, the recruit has committed himself to five years' service, although there is a probationary period to be served. During that period, the recruit may request to leave of his own volition, or the Legion may terminate his employment should it appear that he is unsuited for life in the service. However, the recruit will have to wait before finally committing himself to the Legion; a number of other obstacles have to be cleared at the Legion's headquarters at Aubagne. Until the time comes for him to leave for that base, the recruit will return to his *corvée*, waiting to be taken off to the basic training course.

Basic Training

All new recruits to the Legion are eventually taken from the holding camp at which they are billeted and sent to Aubagne. The first three weeks of life here can be less than exciting; time is taken up with security checks, medicals and aptitude tests and more interviews, plus the inevitable *corvée*. The first three weeks of life with the Legion are likely to be rather boring, but there is a clear purpose to the apparently dull lifestyle: recruits are introduced gradually to Legion life before the rigours of training start.

Recruits are briefly reunited with their belongings on their journey to Aubagne, before surrendering them once more upon arrival. A proper kit issue then takes place, and each new recruit is given a haircut. No matter where they have come from, the recruits (or *Engagés Volontaires* – EVs) are treated as equals, with only the slightest allowances being made for those who cannot speak French. The French-speaking EVs are paired with a man who has little, if any, command of the language, and it is their task to help their new companion to learn. Rapid fluency is not expected, but proficiency is – a legionnaire is of little use if he cannot understand orders. In addition to this 'buddy' system of learning, lessons are provided every day to ensure that the EV's language skills develop quickly.

Alongside his participation in the language training (either as part of the teaching process or as a student), the new recruit is subjected to more tests. The first set of tests are medical. While the recruit will have been given a basic checkup at his holding centre, the tests at Aubagne are more stringent. Blood tests and X-rays are carried out and once the recruit is deemed to meet the required medical standard, he is able to progress to the next stage. This stage involves psychological assessments and intelligence testing. All EVs must score at least 6 out of 20 points, or

Above: Legionnaires stand to attention, waiting to be briefed prior to taking part in an exercise in Corsica, held in October 1981. The legionnaires are aboard a ship, most likely an aircraft carrier, and will probably be deployed to the exercise area by one of the vessel's Super Frelon helicopters.

Above: A legion NCO gives a French language class to legionnaires serving with 13 DBLE in Djibouti. Although all of the students will have been given instruction while undergoing training in France, such tuition is available at each regiment so that recent arrivals can continue to improve their standard of spoken French.

their career with the Legion comes to an abrupt halt. Those scoring 12 points or more in the tests are marked out as potential future non-commissioned officers, although there is obviously far more to gaining promotion than passing tests at the earliest stages of basic training.

Once these tests are successfully negotiated, the EVs are then subjected to close scrutiny by the Legion's security arm, which rejoices in the slightly unlikely name of *Bureau des Statistiques de la Légion* (BSLE). BSLE will put all new recruits through a series of interviews in which the EV's background and past are investigated. The first interview is a simple face-to-face discussion with an NCO, while the second is conducted by a panel. The answers given are subjected to careful scrutiny – the Legion does not need to recruit hardened criminals into its ranks, and any EV who proves to have a serious criminal record is likely to find that his contract is terminated forthwith.

After passing the interview process, the EV begins formal induction into the Legion with a final week at Aubagne. This is pre-ceded with another haircut, this time in the short style favoured by the Legion, the so-called *boule à zero*. By this point, the number of EVs left at Aubagne will have fallen. Some will have chosen to leave, others will have failed the intelligence tests and yet more will have fallen foul of the interviews by BSLE.

Those left face one more week at Aubagne, and this begins with fitting for their own uniforms (as opposed to the used working dress with which they are issued upon arrival at the centre). More aptitude tests to assess suitability for specialist training are carried out during this week, along with organized sport. Towards the end of the final week, the EVs will start to conduct road runs wearing their combat kit for the first time. On the final day, they are provided with their full kit issue, containing most of the items that they will require for the next five years.

All that remains is their signature of the engagement contracts, finally committing the EV to the Legion. Early the next day, the EVs leave Aubagne for Castelnaudary, the base of the *4e Régiment Etranger* (4th Legion Regiment; 4 RE). They shortly discover that their three weeks at Aubagne have been a relatively gentle introduction to life in the Legion – the hard training begins almost immediately upon arrival.

Castelnaudary

New recruits arrive at Castelnaudary early on a Friday morning, and they are formed into sections of between 40 and 50 men, who will embark upon four months of rigorous training. The sections are divided into four groups, three of which will be under the command of a young officer, with the fourth commanded by a *Sous-Officier* (the French term for a senior non-commissioned officer, holding a rank between *sergent* and *major* – the latter not equating to the British and American rank of that title).

The first month is spent acquiring basic military skills and generally acclimatizing the recruit to the way the Legion operates. Unlike other armies, recruits who have an appropriate skill from their civilian life are given the opportunity to use it from the outset. Thus, it is

Above: One of the integral parts of life in the Legion is caring for personal uniform. It is not required for legionnaires to wear their dress uniform when doing their ironing, however, which suggests that this photograph was taken while last-minute preparations for a ceremonial occasion were underway.

Comparative Ranks

The table below shows the comparative ranks between the Legion and the British and US armies.

FRENCH	BRITISH	AMERICAN RANKS
Marechal de France	Field Marshal	General of the Army
General d'Armee	General	General
General de Corps d'Armee	Lieutenant-General	Lieutenant-General
General de Division	Major-General	Major-General
General de Brigade	Brigadier	Brigadier-General
Colonel	Colonel	Colonel
Lieutenant-colonel	Lieutenant-Colonel	Lieutenant-Colonel
Commandant	Major	Major
Capitaine	Captain	Captain
Lieutenant	Lieutenant	First Lieutenant
Sous-lieutenant	Second Lieutenant	Second Lieutenant
Aspirant	(No direct equivalent)	(No direct equivalent)
Major	(No direct equivalent)	(No direct equivalent)
Adjudant-chef	Warrant Officer 1	Chief Warrant Officer
Adjudant	Warrant Officer 2	Warrant Officer Junior
Sergent-major	(No direct equivalent)	First Sergeant
Sergent-chef	Staff Sergeant	Master Sergeant
Sergent	Sergeant	Sergeant First Class
Caporal-chef	(No direct equivalent)	(No direct equivalent)
Caporal	Corporal	Corporal
Soldat (legionnaire) de 1ére classe	Lance Corporal	Private First Class
Soldat (legionnaire) de 2e classe	Private	Private

Opposite: Legionnaires on parade. Formal parades are another key part of Legion life, and cover everything from the start of guard duty to big regimental occasions such as Camerone Day. The frequency of such parades means that the legionnaires are kept busy making sure that their uniform is in spotless condition.

common for a former chef to be given the task of cooking for his section, while those qualified to drive goods vehicles will serve as section drivers, taking their colleagues to and from the training ground.

The recruits also find that their accommodation is rather better than that 'enjoyed' by recruits in many other armies, since they are billeted on one of the three farms owned by the Legion's training regiment. Each farm, despite an old, rustic-looking exterior, is well appointed, with central heating and full-scale washing and cooking facilities. This standard was not always the case, however, and until the late 1980s the farms were rather run down, with leaking roofs and poor facilities. (Some former legionnaires have suggested that the old, uncomfortable quarters were excellent preparation for life on operations, and bemoan the fact that training has 'gone soft'.) Each 10-man group has its own dormitory, while their NCOs have separate accommodation nearby.

If the recruits have not understood the Legion's near obsession with keeping everywhere clean and tidy from the amount of *corvée* undertaken while waiting to go to Castelnaudary, they soon learn, as they are expected to keep their dormitories in pristine condition.

Above: A Japanese volunteer is pictured in his quarters. The basic nature of the accommodation is notable, although it will be kept as clean and tidy as possible. The proliferation of items on the wall and floor suggest that this billet is lacking storage lockers. Accommodation for legionnaires has improved considerably in the last 20 years.

First Phase Training

The first phase of training is largely devoted to physical fitness and military discipline. While the Legion no longer makes use of corporal punishment or threatens miscreants in as brutal a fashion as it once did, the slightest infraction is likely to result in some additional physical strain. Standards in all things are expected to be high, and it becomes very obvious to the recruit that he must begin to gain some command of the French language if he cannot speak it already. Perhaps of equal importance, the legionnaire must start to learn the rank structure of the Legion, so as to avoid incurring the wrath of someone senior whom he has forgotten to salute.

One of the most important facets of the Legion's rank structure is the fact that all those above the rank of *sergent* are saluted by their subordinates. This differs from the practice in most other armies where it is only officers who are entitled to 'compliments' from those below them (although only the very unwise would risk being disrespectful to their non-commissioned officers).

The French practice means that recruits find themselves doing a great deal of saluting, as they will come into contact with *sergents* quite frequently during the course of their day. Rank etiquette is further complicated by the fact that a salute is only expected on the first meeting each day between senior and junior.

Former legionnaires have observed that trying to remember whom they had saluted and whom they had not was a source of some distraction as they attempted to do everything correctly, and not find themselves facing the displeasure of their senior (although those who did not receive a salute were far more irritated than those mistakenly saluted for a second time).

The Legion also expects that legionnaires will adopt a rather prescriptive means of addressing their superiors when in a formal setting (for instance, an interview), known as *la presentation*. The legionnaire must remember to follow a series of moves and phrases as he meets his superior. This series begins with the legionnaire keeping his eyes fixed on his superior, then standing to attention and saluting, next removing headgear (left hand only) before informing the superior of the legionnaire's name, length of

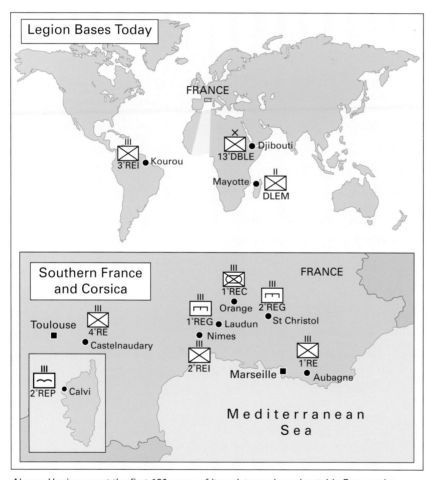

Above: Having spent the first 130 years of its existence based outside France, the Legion's forces are preponderantly in the mother country, with some outposts overseas. The only full-size unit abroad is 3 REI in Guiana, with a Demi-Brigade in Djibouti along with some involvement in a small detachment in Mayotte. The rest of the Legion's forces are based in the southern part of France and Corsica – a far cry from the days when the Legion was based abroad with the aim of preventing foreign soldiers from running amok in mainland France.

service and assignment within the unit. The superior then invites the legionnaire to stand at ease, at which point the legionnaire tells the superior rank that he 'stands at ease at your command, Sir'. A similar procedure is followed when the legionnaire is dismissed. Although this process seems rather over-formal to many, it is something that the Legion expects, and which is followed scrupulously. It should be noted that in less formal settings, the legionnaire is not expected to follow this procedure, but he is at least expected to come to attention and salute when approaching a superior.

Similar high standards are expected when a recruit or fully fledged legionnaire is detailed to carry out guard duty. A very formalized procedure is in place for the changing of the guard, involving bugles and the raising of the French flag, and even when this is negotiated, the guards must show the most punctilious standards of dress and deportment throughout daylight hours.

As night falls, the guards change into standard combat uniform. They sleep in this uniform, ready to respond if called out, and it is not until their 24-hour stint of guard duty is over that they can relax a little. However, even then it does not mean that the legionnaire has nothing to do; once off guard duty, a whole array of domestic chores need to be carried out.

A number of former legionnaires have commented that they were thoroughly sick of mops and buckets by the time they left the Legion, since *corvée* duties are something that affect recruits and legionnaires alike until they are

The Legion Today

1er Régiment Etranger (1st Legion Regiment; 1 RE)
Founded: 1841 Base: Aubagne

4e Régiment Etranger (4th Legion Regiment; 4 RE)
Founded: 1920 Base: Castelnaudary

1er Régiment Etranger de Cavalerie
(1st Legion Cavalry Regiment; 1 REC)
Founded: 1921 Base: Orange

1er Régiment Etranger de Génie
(1st Legion Engineer Regiment; 1 REG)
Founded: 1984 Base: Laudun

2e Régiment Etranger d'Infanterie
(2nd Legion Infantry Regiment; 2 REI)
Founded: 1841 Base: Nimes

2e Régiment Etranger de Genie
(2nd Legion Engineer Regiment; 2 REG)
Founded: 1999 Base: Saint Christol

2e Régiment Etranger de Parachutistes
(2nd Legion Parachute Regiment; 2 REP)
Founded: 1948 Base: Calvi (Corsica)

3e Régiment Etranger d'Infanterie
(3rd Legion Infantry Regiment; 3 REI)
Founded: 1920 Base: Kourou (French Guiana)

13e Demi-Brigade de Légion Etrangère
(13th Legion Demi-Brigade; 13 DBLE)
Founded: 1940 Base: Djibouti

Détachement de Légion Etrangère de Mayotte
(Legion Detachment Mayotte)
Founded: 1976 Base: Dzaoudzi (Mayotte)

Strength of the Legion (September 2004):
408 Officers
1724 Non-Commissioned Officers
5530 Legionnaires

Above: A legionnaire makes sure that his képi is correctly adjusted before reporting for duty at the guardhouse. Unlike many other units, the Legion expects those carrying out guard duty to be in parade dress. This means that those on the main gate present a smart image to members of the public passing by, something considered of importance by the Legion.

promoted to non-commissioned rank (although even then it is likely that they will find themselves supervising such chores).

Desertion

Coupled with the hard nature of the training and the drudgery of the *corvée*, the scrupulous formality and constant high standards required may be factors in prompting some recruits to desert. The fact that the recruits may not be allowed contact with their families for the first two months of training can add to a sense of isolation and discontent, and it is not uncommon

for any of these factors, or a combination thereof, to convince the recruit that he has made a mistake, and that he wishes to escape life as a legionnaire.

When training at the Legion's farms, it is relatively easy for a recruit to desert, since he does not have to negotiate guards or fences to leave. The instructors pay careful attention to the numbers of recruits in front of them throughout the day, since it is not uncommon for would-be deserters to disappear when the instructor's back is turned. The Legion takes a dim view of those who desert, or more

accurately those who desert and who are recaptured.

However, the Legion does not always find it easy to track down those who have left before the end of their contract, and this fact means that would-be deserters are not deterred from fleeing. It is easy to overstate how prevalent desertion is, but it is a constant problem that the Legion has to face. It is not just recruits who are prone to departing without permission, but also legionnaires with some years of service behind them. In some cases, deserters return to their home country and join (or rejoin) the armed forces there. This can create some interesting situations for deserters from NATO member countries should the deserter find himself working alongside the Legion when his new unit is on exercise in France, or on deployment alongside the Legion as part of an overseas NATO mission. In one case, a British paratrooper, a deserter from the Legion, found himself living alongside his former colleagues on an exercise; in another, a Legion deserter who had been commissioned in the armed forces of his own country ended up working with one of his officers from his time in the Legion.

Although the Legion would perhaps have been entitled to try to take steps to reclaim their lost legionnaires (on the basis that they now knew where they were), a diplomatic blind eye was turned.

In other cases, should the deserter be found, he may be returned to the Legion, given a spell of imprisonment and then forced to complete his five-year contract. Despite this sanction, the Legion considers taking such a step carefully, since it may well be the case that the deserter, if forced back into the Legion for a few years, may be a disruptive influence. It is increasingly common for the deserter to be placed under arrest, inconvenienced for a few weeks or months either in military prison or carrying out tedious fatigue duties at a Legion base and then dismissed from the Legion.

Marching and Road Runs

Those recruits not tempted to desert (the majority) discover that much of their time is taken up with marching, inspections and drills,

and they do not have much opportunity to sleep. The EVs become familiar with road runs at Aubagne, but those at Castelnaudary are longer, more frequent and generally tougher. The runs become more taxing as training progresses, and recruits are driven hard. Recruits can find themselves marching for 50km (31 miles) in full kit, or having to complete a cross-country run in under an hour. During the marches, spirits are maintained by singing. The Legion lays great store in such vocal activity, not only because it helps morale and team spirit, but because it is a useful mechanism to assist non-French speakers to acquire the language. The Legion's attachment to singing is demonstrated by the fact that the Legion song-book is

published. One former legionnaire has observed that there is one drawback to many of the songs, since they seem to be concerned with death or defeat, which is hardly conducive to morale.

The first phase of training concludes after a month with a 50km (31-mile) march from the farms back to Castelnaudary. The recruits carry a full rucksack, which seems to become heavier with every step as the march unfolds. The climate in the south of France ensures that the weather is often unbearably hot for the recruits, and the march becomes a true test of endurance. When the march is over, the recruit is entitled to wear the Legion's famed *képi blanc*.

The presentation ceremony is quite simple: the recruits assemble,

Above: Legionnaires undertake a road run in full kit as dusk falls. The Legion's training consists of a great deal of roadwork. Although training is rather less brutal in terms of discipline than it used to be, the physical exertion required remains considerable.

Above: Two legionnaires practice their unarmed combat skills. Such training is carried out in as realistic a manner as possible, and it is rare for legionnaires to return to barracks without having picked up a few cuts and bruises.

képis in hand, before their section officer. The officer issues the word of command, at which point the recruits don the *képi* and burst into song. This is a moment of much pride for the recruits, but does not mean that they are near to the end of their training.

Second Phase Training

The EVs now enter the second phase of their training, which begins to introduce more rigorous military discipline than seen before. Individual appearance starts to assume greater importance, and the training NCOs pay close attention to standards of dress – having received the *képi blanc*, the EVs are expected to look like fully fledged legionnaires. They also discover that the training becomes more intense, with basic weapons training appearing on the syllabus. The legionnaire becomes acquainted with the standard French service rifle, the FAMAS. As well as learning how to handle the weapon, the recruits spend time on the range each day, their shooting practice interspersed with French language training, physical fitness and drill.

The standards expected of the recruits are high, although those who fail to achieve them are not subjected to some of the more brutal punishments of the past. When the Legion was based in Algeria, it was not uncommon for miscreants to be buried up to their necks in the desert sand with no protection from the sun. Slightly less extreme physical punishment included being struck over the head with a rifle or punched by the NCO conducting the instruction.

Some NCOs seemed to enjoy brutality, and this often led to diffi-

Above: A member of 2 REP negotiates a river obstacle while carrying out jungle training in Guiana. The Legion benefits from having large overseas bases that make it possible for all members of the unit to receive regular training in different environments, adding to the versatility of the soldiers.

culties – NCOs sometimes found that the target of their attacks responded in kind (although such retaliation usually led to even more punishment), and it has been suggested that some legionnaires, tired of their bullying NCOs, simply did away with them. Another response to such treatment was desertion.

Although the Legion now frowns upon the use of physical punishment (although it is a fact that some NCOs still endeavour to employ it), the strict discipline in training and beyond ensures that desertion remains a problem the Legion fights to control.

Although the Legion constantly reinforces discipline, it would be wrong to suggest that the training is a monotonous regime. The second phase of training ends with a visit to the Legion base at Camurac in the Pyrenees. In the winter the recruits will be provided with instruction in skiing and cold-weather fighting techniques, while those attending in summer are taught the basic skills needed for rock climbing. As part of the rock-climbing course, the recruits are given the opportunity to abseil from the nearby cliffs. In general, recruits enjoy the training at Camurac, but this phase is marked by another hard march at its conclusion. The recruits are expected to march, with full equipment, some 60-70km (37-43 miles). This is the hardest march that the recruits have faced to date, and it marks the end of the second phase of their training.

Third Phase Training

The third phase of training is designed to enhance the tactical

Above: A legionnaire carries out a barrel change on his AAT-52 general purpose machine gun while training on the ranges. The man behind him carries a short length of link ammunition for the weapon threaded through his belt. The AAT-52 is still employed by the Legion, although it is steadily being replaced by the FN Minimi at section level.

skills of the recruits, putting together some of the earlier aspects of training. The recruits are taught fire-and-manoeuvre tactics, and make use of a wider range of weapons than before. Grenades, anti-tank weapons and heavy machine guns are all introduced into the regime as the volunteers begin the transition from raw recruits to trained legionnaires. The recruits are also introduced to the basic skills required for night-fighting, gaining some understanding of the fundamental difficulties of navigating in low-light conditions and identifying targets in the dark.

While these skills are being developed, the recruits continue to be subjected to fitness training. The marching becomes harder and longer and they are faced with more difficult terrains. Some of the basic route marches can last for three days, with nights under canvas. The pace is relentless, but by this stage the recruits are almost universally determined to battle on, since to drop out and fail would involve letting down their section as well as call into question their future as a legionnaire.

As the third phase progresses, the non-French-speaking recruits start to find their adopted language easier – they may not be fluent, but they can at least make themselves understood by their colleagues and, perhaps more importantly, they are able to understand exactly what it is that their instructors expect them to do.

As training enters its fourth and final month, the recruits are subjected to a range of assessments. These evaluations are partly to ensure that the recruit has digested all that he has learned, and partly to

determine where in the Legion the man will be sent at the end of training. Once completed, the recruits will be considered to have passed their *Certificat Technique Elémentaire*, or CTE/00, the benchmark for their proficiency as legionnaires. A three-day exercise tests all the skills the recruits have learned over the course of their training, and calls for a march of some 150km (93 miles), followed by a raid on an 'enemy' position.

When the exercise is completed, the EVs are then expected to complete the *cent cartouches* (One Hundred Rounds) test. As the name suggests, the recruit is provided with 100 rounds of live ammunition, which he must use to demonstrate his proficiency with his rifle. Once this test is over, the recruit faces a series of examinations covering everything from radio procedure to the use of machine guns and anti-tank weapons. In addition to these practical tests, the EV is expected to display a thorough knowledge of the field manual. As soon as the recruit is deemed to have met the requisite standard, he is awarded his CTE/00. Once he is presented with this certificate, training is over – the recruit is now a legionnaire.

Entry
The newly qualified legionnaires then return to Castelnaudary to begin entry into the Legion proper. They are subjected to more medical tests to ensure that they are fully fit, and while they are waiting, they apply for the posting that they wish to take up.

Postings are arranged by the simple expedient of all the Legion's regiments providing a list of vacan-

cies in their ranks. The Legion tries to ensure that every man is posted to the place he wishes to go, so as to avoid disgruntled new legionnaires arriving at their regiments. In cases where vacancies do not exist, it is not uncommon for the Legion to show a certain degree of flexibility: the legionnaire will be told that he will be unable to go to his preferred posting for some months, and is sent on a temporary attachment to another regiment. Alternatively, the staff at Castelnaudary will make informal contact with the commanding officer of the regiment in question to see if an extra place can be found for the eager new legionnaire. Invariably, a place is found.

Having applied for their postings, the legionnaires then return to Aubagne, where their journey began. They wait until their posting is confirmed, and then set out to join their new regiment. The staff at Aubagne take the opportunity to make sure that the legionnaire really wishes to commit himself for five years, and in some cases, he will admit that he does not, and would like to leave. Although such men represent a frustrating waste of training effort (and money), it is considered better to let them go, since they are unlikely to make committed soldiers. However, if a legionnaire does not avail himself of this opportunity, he is deemed to have committed himself to the contract, and only in rare instances will he be permitted to leave before the end of his term of service. Having fully entered the Legion, the new man awaits his posting, which can be either in France itself, or to one of the French outposts thousands of miles away.

Le Boudin

Although the Foreign Legion has an array of songs stretching back to its formation, the most important is *Le Boudin*. This is perhaps one of the most unusual song choices for a military unit, since it is not about some tale of derring-do, or, indeed, anything eventful in the Legion's history: it is, in fact, about black pudding (better known in some countries as blood sausage).

Tiens, voila du boudin,
voila du boudin,
voila du boudin
Pour les Alsaciens, les Suisses, et les Lorrains
Pour les Belges, il n'y en a plus,
pour les Belges, il n'y en a plus
Ce sont des tireurs au cul. Tireurs au cul.

Well, there's sausage,
There's sausage,
There's sausage
For the Alsatians, the Swiss and the Lorrainers
For the Belgians there's none left,
for the Belgians there's none left
They are idlers. Idlers.

A number of legionnaires who have tasted *Le Boudin* have expressed the view that the Belgians mentioned in the song had a lucky escape.

Joining a Regiment

The legionnaire has a variety of possible postings he can apply for. There are eight Legion regiments, although a freshly trained legionnaire is very unlikely to join 4 RE given its training role, and joining 1 RE does not involve a great deal of travelling to get to the new posting. For those who have just finished training, and who are at Aubagne already, joining 1 RE may seem unadventurous, but it is regarded as a reasonable first posting, albeit not one to stay in for all five years of the contract if at all possible.

Apart from 1 RE, there are four regiments in mainland France. These consist of the *1er Régiment Etranger de Cavalerie* (1st Legion Cavalry Regiment; 1 REC), the *2e Régiment Etranger d'Infanterie* (2nd Legion Infantry Regiment; 2 REI) and two *Régiment Etranger de Genie* (engineering regiments) – 1 REG and 2 REG. The first three named units form part of *6e Division Légère Blindée* (6th Light Armoured Division; 6 DLB), while 2 REG is a component of the *27e Brigade D'Infanterie de Montagne* (27th Mountain Brigade; 27 BIM).

The 6 DLB is part of the French rapid-reaction force, the *Force d'Action Rapide* (FAR). The FAR contains more than just the Legion's regiments, but the Legion provides the force with a considerable part of its fighting strength.

The 1 REC contributes up to 48 armoured reconnaissance vehicles in the form of AMX-10RC armoured cars (although unlike most armoured cars, the AMX-10RC sports a 105mm (4in) gun that is capable of troubling enemy tanks), while 2 REI is one of the formation's two infantry regiments. Combat engineering duties for the FAR are the purview of 1 REG, which has been with the force since 1984 (although it was known as 6 REG until 1999).

2e Régiment Etranger de Parachutistes

If joining one of the units in FAR does not appeal, the legionnaire may be tempted to join possibly the most glamorous of the Legion's units, namely the *2e Régiment Etranger de Parachutistes* (2nd Legion Parachute Regiment; 2 REP). Based at Calvi in Corsica, 2 REP seems to offer legionnaires the

best chance of seeing active service during their five years. Since parachutists receive additional pay in the French Army (a common practice in airborne units), joining 2 REP offers both excitement and improved finances.

Because 2 REP is an attractive posting, this allows the regiment to be selective, and prospective parachutists must have performed well in the intelligence tests they received at the outset of their career in the Legion (this does not stop 2 REP from putting aspiring paratroopers through another similar test, however). As well as

appearing to be an 'elite within an elite' in the eyes of some, 2 REP also contains its own special operations force. The force used to operate under the name of *Commandos de Recherche et d'Action dans la Profondeur* (CRAP). The resulting acronym is unfortunate to the eyes and ears of English speakers, but was hardly an appropriate description of the quality of the force. Sadly for those wishing to joke about the acronym, the commandos underwent a reorganization at the end of the 1990s, and were re-titled as the *Groupement de Commandos*

Above: Members of 2 REP's 4th Company prepare to go out in the field for an exercise. The Legion makes considerable use of snipers, not least since experience has shown that the suppressive fire that they can bring to bear is most useful in peacekeeping and rescue operations. The snipers are also a valuable tool for carrying out covert reconnaissance.

Parachutistes (GCP). The new legionnaire is not able to undergo selection for the GCP at the start of his career, but it is something that a number of legionnaires aspire to do after they have gained more experience (invariably when they are on their second five-year contract). Although legionnaires joining 2 REP undergo further intensive training to prepare them for the parachute role, they are not alone in facing yet more training when they join their unit.

Postings

Those who head for 3 REI in French Guiana are sent to the Equatorial Forest Training Centre to equip them for life in the region. The new arrivals face a rigorous course that trains them for operations in the jungle, a unique environment with particular challenges for soldiering.

A similarly exotic yet challenging location awaits those posted to *13e Demi-Brigade de Légion Etrangère* (13th Legion Demi-Brigade; 13 DBLE), a half-brigade based in Djibouti. The 13 DBLE is a mixed-arms unit, containing a headquarters and support company, a rifle company, an armoured reconnaissance squadron as well as a company of engineers. In addition to these permanently based units, 13 DBLE usually has a company supplied by 2 REP (on a rotational basis) to bolster its strength. A Djibouti posting requires legionnaires to be familiar with desert warfare, a skill with which the Legion has been identified from its earliest days. In more recent times, the core skills learned by the Legion from its posting in Djibouti have been put to good use in Chad and in the 1991 Gulf War.

Those legionnaires based in mainland France may not need similarly strenuous training to ensure that they can operate in the local environment, but this does not mean that they are left with little of interest to do.

As a cavalry regiment, 1 REC retains a certain amount of glamour associated with the days when cavalry units had horses rather than armour, and were

Above: Members of 1 RE practice their bayonet drill in the Saudi Arabian desert while preparing for participation in Operation Desert Storm (known as Operation Daguet to the French).

famed for their dash and élan. 1 REC tries to maintain these qualities as it trains new legionnaires in the subtleties of operating armoured vehicles and the techniques required for successful missions. Although 1 REC has vehicles that can deal with enemy tanks, its main function is as a reconnaissance formation.

As such, it is usually regarded as a bad idea for the AMX-10RCs to seek contact with the enemy for the purpose of engaging them in battle. Despite the traditional flair expected of a cavalry regiment, professionalism demands that some discretion is shown when reconnoitring, to ensure that the mission is not compromised.

The 2 REI and the two engineer regiments may appear to lack the glamour and toughness associated with 2 REP and 1 REC and may not offer the exotic locations of the units based aboard. Their tasks, however, are equally important, and rigorous training is carried out to ensure that they are an effective part of the reaction force. Also, while a legionnaire may not start his career as a paratrooper, there is nothing to prevent him from joining 2 REP later.

By contrast, members of 2 REP may find themselves posted elsewhere later in their careers as the Legion seeks to ensure that no one formation becomes insular and its members dedicated to a single specialization.

Such cross-posting is in keeping with the notion of the Legion as being one large family, where all legionnaires are more or less equal and required to undertake a number of roles. The point about the Legion as family is something

Above: A legionnaire stands guard over AMX-10RC reconnaissance vehicles belonging to 1 REC while deployed on peacekeeping operations in the Bosnian canton of Tomislavgrad during the summer of 1995.

drilled into legionnaires from their first day with the organization, and they are not permitted to forget this fact. Although their membership of the 'family' begins in training, it becomes very real to the new legionnaire upon posting to his first regimental duties.

These begin with the specialized training required so that the legionnaire can play a full and meaningful part in the role assigned to the regiment, be that parachuting, armoured reconnaissance, combat engineering or the light infantry role.

Specialization: Training and Skills of the Legion

Although all legionnaires are subjected to rigorous basic and further training, they will each be given an additional military speciality. Their speciality equips them with the necessary skills for working with the regiment, and ensures that their abilities are maintained at a high level.

Detailing the different specialist training within each Legion regiment would almost fill an entire book in its own right. This chapter, therefore, addresses some of the specialist training commonly available to legionnaires (including extreme terrain training), and then concentrates in more detail on the training for the parachute, commando and anti-terrorist roles that the Legion undertakes.

Looking at *2e Régiment Etranger de Parachutistes* (2nd Legion Parachute Regiment; 2 REP) is useful, since the regiment's six companies each have a specific role that encompasses the specialist training available to the Legion as a whole.

Para Training

After the legionnaire has completed his four months of basic training at Castelnaudary, and has volunteered for 2 REP, he is sent to the regimental base at Calvi. On arrival at Camp Raffalli, the legionnaire will be met by the corporal assigned to the next parachute course and taken to a billet. Parachute courses are run on a

regular basis, and they are not dependent upon having a certain number of men available before they can take place. The course involves a mixture of physical

fitness training, to provide the necessary upper-body strength required for manoeuvring a parachute, along with instruction about the equipment and jumping proce-

Above: Members of 6 REG, the Legion's engineer regiment in the early 1990s, practice mine-clearance during a training exercise in France.

Right: Members of 2 REP carry out a practice parachute drop during Exercise Winged Crusader, 1993. 2 REP often deploy to exercises via parachute, since although they are just as likely to arrive at their objective by helicopter, vehicle or on foot, the ability to parachute into a combat zone remains immensely valuable, as demonstrated at Kolwezi.

dures employed. The physical training is an important factor, since none of the new recruits to 2 REP are forced to undergo a fitness test before they are accepted. This means that some of the new arrivals find it necessary to work particularly hard on their conditioning to meet the highest standards required of parachutists. Once the legionnaire has received sufficient instruction in the use of the equipment, the practical side of parachute training begins.

To receive his parachutist's 'wings', the legionnaire must complete six jumps. Calvi is an ideal place for parachute training, since the drop zone for the paratroopers is located alongside the 2 REP base, and only a matter of miles away from the airfield. This positioning allows fairly intensive training to take place, since the legionnaires can be removed from the drop zone, taken back to the airfield and do another training jump all within the space of a couple of hours.

There is, however, a penalty associated with this convenience – the drop zone's proximity to the 2 REP camp can make for some interesting landings for those who do not steer their parachutes precisely enough. In the past, legionnaires have been known to land back in the camp rather than on the drop zone, and this also means that

training cannot be carried out when the wind rises, so an alternative drop zone on the other side of the island is used.

The first phase of the training is designed to familiarize the new arrivals with their equipment and how to use it properly. The drills

required for parachuting must be instinctive, and the training is intense. The legionnaires begin with a simple introduction to the parachute, the so-called 'naming of parts'. At the end of this, the legionnaire will know what every part of his parachute is, and what it does;

Above: Members of 2 REP share the back of the aircraft carrying with them a 120mm (4.9in) mortar. Although paratroops are traditionally lightly-equipped, weapons of this size are of great utility in providing heavy firepower, as are air-portable howitzers.

they will also have the first notion of what they need to do if one of the parts goes wrong while they are hanging beneath the parachute. One of the key skills to be learned from the outset is how to land properly. The instructors will show their charges how to land and roll, insisting that they practice landing rolls on a regular basis. Legionnaires can end the day bruised and aching having carried out hundreds of practice rolls, with the instructors forcing them to repeat the activity if they do not do it absolutely correctly.

Having mastered the art of landing, the would-be paratroopers are taught more basic skills, such as how to board the transport aircraft – more difficult than it sounds when loaded down with a parachute, reserve parachute and a full rucksack – and then the correct method of leaving the aircraft when about to jump. Jump procedure can be more difficult in reality than might be appreciated – the parachutist must ensure that the static line (the means by which the parachute will be deployed) is not across his body, since this could strangle him as he leaves the aircraft; he must stand in the door correctly and then force himself out so as to avoid being blown back into the airframe by the slipstream. Although the journey down may give a grandstand view of the countryside beneath, only the most unwise paratrooper will admire the view, as there is a considerable danger of collision with other parachutists.

Before the prospective paratrooper is allowed to try his newly acquired skills for real, he will go to the training area to practice on hanging harnesses, mock-up aircraft and a landing tower. The hanging harness is employed so that the trainee can, as the name of the apparatus suggests, hang in a parachute harness as if he had just jumped from an aircraft and was beneath the open canopy. He can then learn the necessary techniques for controlling the parachute, along with appropriate emergency drills. The landing tower is a more formidable piece of apparatus, standing about 10m (32ft) high.

The recruit hangs in a parachute harness and adopts the landing position. On a word of command from an instructor, the weight holding the parachute harness (and the recruit) aloft is released and the trainee drops rapidly towards the ground, just as he would in a real landing. The legionnaire then does his best to land properly – feet together, legs bending into the landing and then rolling over.

After two weeks of this instruction (always interspersed with runs and physical training), the recruits are deemed ready to take their first jump. The legionnaires board a French Air Force transport aircraft (usually a Transall C.160, but occasionally a C-130 Hercules) and are flown towards the drop zone. Frequently, one of the instructors will order his charges to begin singing, partly out of the Legion habit of breaking into song when an opportunity presents itself, and partly to distract the men from what lies ahead. After a few minutes, the aircraft will begin its run-in to the drop zone.

A few miles away from the point where the men will jump out, the aircraft loadmaster begins to issue instructions. The parachutists clamber to their feet and shuffle towards the side exits of the aircraft. They hook up to the release cable that will automatically deploy the parachutes once the static-line connection between parachute and release cable goes taut, whipping the parachute out of its pack.

The legionnaire will check the position of the static line so that it is not crossing in front of his neck, or if he does not, the loadmaster will notice and position him correctly. The exit door is opened, and as soon as the aircraft is in the correct alignment with the drop zone, the pilot will signal to the loadmaster (and all those in the cargo bay) by use of the traditional light indicators: a red light comes on above the door to show that the run-in to the drop zone has begun, and then at the correct moment, the light will change to green, and the loadmasters order the paratroops out into space. During his descent the legionnaire will run through the necessary drills and any corrective actions required. Has his canopy opened correctly? Is he about to collide with any of his colleagues? Is he in the right position to land on the drop zone? Almost before he is aware of it, he will be landing.

The legionnaire must then endeavour to release his parachute so that he is not dragged along the ground by it, and once free must then gather in the canopy so that it can be returned to the parachute store. The legionnaire must repeat this experience six times, including once at night, once simulating the failure of the main canopy and using the reserve parachute, and once carrying full equipment.

2 REP in the 1960s

For 2 REP, the 1960s began with the war in Algeria, in which they fought a series of small, frustrating actions against ALN guerrillas, aware that General de Gaulle's government intended to bring an end to French rule. Their colleagues in 1 REP launched an abortive coup attempt in April 1961. This failed after a week, and 1 REP was promptly disbanded. Many of the officers were arrested and dismissed, while those who were not were dispersed, along with their men, through the rest of the Legion. This left 2 REP as the only Legion parachute regiment. Morale throughout the Legion was low, but the bond between the paratroopers meant that in 2 REP was notably poor. Matters improved when Lieutenant-Colonel Caillaud arrived to take command in 1963. He determined to change 2 REP from a parachute infantry regiment into a versatile parachute-commando unit that could be deployed rapidly around the world. His plan led to the formation of 2 REP as it is today, with individual companies mastering a particular area of expertise. Caillaud's plan worked – as 2 REP trained, morale soared, and within two years, morale was at such a level that re-enlistment rates were amongst the highest in the Legion. Once 2 REP moved to Corsica, it was assigned to the 11th Division for rapid deployment overseas.

Above: Two legionnaires from 2 REP practise close-quarter fighting. Both are wearing respirators to protect against the effect of CS gas that would be used to disorientate the occupants of the building. The man on the left is carrying a pump-action shotgun, useful for removing doors from their hinges, while the soldier on the right carries a suppressed MP5 submachine gun.

When the six jumps have been successfully completed, the legionnaire is awarded his parachutist's wings by the commanding officer of the training centre, while a senior NCO attaches the regimental lanyard to the shoulder of the newly inducted paratrooper.

Continuation and Specialization

The legionnaire now goes on to develop a specialized skill within 2 REP. The regiment has five companies, each with a different opera-

tional capability. Specialization was brought into being during the 1960s as the Legion's role changed from that of colonial policing to one that could be employed on a whole range of missions.

Although the legionnaire is asked which of the five companies he would like to join at the end of his training and 2 REP will do its best to send him to his preferred company, the legionnaire will be sent where he is needed most. 1st Company of 2 REP has three role specializations. Originally, it was tasked with anti-

tank missions and night fighting, but in the last 10 years or so it has added skills in urban operations, skills that are in much demand for peacekeeping duties. The urban techniques taught include deploying into a city block by abseiling from helicopters and the use of dog teams to search buildings. The talents of 1st Company proved particularly useful in the former Republic of Yugoslavia, when most of the work was conducted in built-up areas. To train for urban operations, the legionnaires of 1st

Company will use a variety of combat ranges in France and allied nations – the urban training centre at Hammelburg in Germany is a favoured venue. Much time is spent on building-clearance actions. The legionnaires learn means of breaking into a fortified building and the easiest way to take a building in urban combat – from the top downwards, rather than fighting their way in through the front door.

Alternative methods of entry are taught, including the use of explosives. Blasting 'mouseholes' through the wall separating rooms is a useful means of surprising the enemy, who is most likely to expect his adversary to effect an entry through the door or window, rather than through the wall. The legionnaires also develop the awareness needed for fighting through a house, such as the need to keep constant surveillance above, behind and to the side, since the enemy may well be hiding in the roof space or be in a room that has not yet been cleared. As well as learning how to break into an occupied building and clear the enemy from it, the legionnaires train to defend a building in the face of an enemy assault. They learn the best way of fortifying a building and setting up firing positions for a variety of weapons, so that a small group of men can use such a position to hold an enemy off for some time.

As well as urban fighting skills, 1st Company receives riot-control training. This training is particularly useful for peacekeeping scenarios when it may be necessary to break up demonstrations by supporters of warring factions. Anti-riot operations have been particularly rele-

vant in the Balkans, where the implementation of the peace accords has been accompanied by rioting by Serbian, Bosnian and Kosovan communities, with their anger directed either towards one another, or sometimes at the peacekeepers themselves.

Finally, 5th Platoon of 1st Company is responsible for training and looking after the regimental dogs. The platoon is made up of 14 handlers and their dogs, and has three specific tasks. The first duty is that of guarding equipment, buildings and personnel. The second task is that of assisting in maintaining law and order (experience has shown that rioters often lose interest in causing trouble when confronted by a legionnaire with an irritated Alsatian), while the third role is in urban fighting.

The dogs are not used as 'weapons' in this latter situation, since it would be a simple task for an armed enemy to shoot the dog as it attacked. Rather, the dogs are employed to locate the enemy, who in a built-up environment has a range of hiding places. Once the dog has found where the enemy is, the handler and dog withdraw and the legionnaires from the other platoons will then prosecute the engagement.

2nd Company

2nd Company of 2 REP specializes in mountain warfare. This means being able to operate in the extreme conditions found in mountainous areas, and the demands of the role mean that even within 2 REP, 2nd Company has something of a reputation for toughness. The legionnaire is expected to undergo a three-week training course to

achieve his 'BAM' – the *Brevet Alpin Militaire* – a gruelling test of endurance. The BAM test is a rapid climb on Mount Cinto, undertaken at the height of summer.

A legionnaire must cover 15km (9 miles) in less than three-and-a-half hours. This is complicated by the fact that the 15km (9 miles) involve a climb and descent of more than 1000m (3280ft). If the feat were not hard enough, the soldiers all carry full rucksacks. One legionnaire recalled that when he carried out the test, 15 of the 26 members of his section crossed the finish line, collapsed and were given fluids intravenously by the medical team.

BAM is not the only test of endurance faced by the members of 2nd Company. Another test is a long route march. The march is along the *Sentier de Grande Randonnée* (otherwise known as GR20), a 149km (93-mile) hiking route, possibly the most difficult of its type in France. The same legionnaire whose section required 15 intravenous drips at the end of the BAM test, ruefully recalled the experience as being 'pure hell', noting that while hikers usually complete the route in 10 days, it was regarded as being bad form for 2nd Company members to take anywhere near as long. Some section staff aimed to complete the entire route in five days. Again, the presence of an extremely heavy pack only added to the pain of the task. In the winter 2nd Company must take the BSM (*Brevet de Skieur Militaire*). The first week of this test is dedicated to teaching the legionnaires to ski.

Once this has been completed (and there are inevitably some legionnaires who do not fully

Above: Members of 2 REP cross a fence as they leave their drop zone. The bulk of their back-packs gives some idea of the heavy loads that paratroopers are required to carry. Note that the man on the extreme left has an AT-4 anti-tank rocket in his rucksack.

master the art in a week), the troops move on to mountain warfare techniques. The two aspects are brought together in a tactical exercise in the third week. The BSM is another serious test of endurance. Once completed, the legionnaire can be considered combat-ready within the company, although further training, including parachuting into snowy terrain, is carried out almost continuously.

3rd Company

The 3rd Company's specialization is amphibious assault. The company's task is to carry out coastal reconnaissance and the capture of beaches as a prelude to an amphibious attack by a larger force. The training for the company is quite involved, since legionnaires need to learn the techniques required of a reconnaissance diver, and how to handle the Zodiac rubber boats in which the company deploys.

The elementary diving test, conducted at the army diving school at Angers, takes 13 weeks, and further qualifications in the field can be taken at a later stage: the course for the most advanced divers lasts for a whole year. As well as learning how to dive and carry out reconnaissance missions, those qualified to the more advanced level will be proficient in using kayaks to make silent approaches to enemy-held beaches. Although the company's divers may be called upon to fight their way out from a beach, they are not combat divers. These are specialists who can carry out a range of demolition tasks as well as reconnaissance missions, and are under the control of the French Navy.

Boat handling courses are similarly demanding, and the end of the training course exercise involves a tour around Corsica in the Zodiacs, carrying out practice approaches to beaches and landing raiding parties. Further specialist training includes learning to parachute into the sea from both aircraft and helicopters and deploying divers from submarines.

All of these skills are brought together in training exercises throughout the year, with one or two large exercises carried out with the Navy. Despite the fact that the company specializes in amphibious operations, it is still able to perform infantry operations, and has carried out its fair share of peacekeeping duties in recent years, frequently at distances considerably removed from the coast.

4th Company

The 4th Company takes the title of 'Destruction and Sniper Company'. While the latter part has self-evident meaning, the 'destruction' part of the name refers to the company's responsibility for demolition operations, particularly behind enemy lines. Members of the company are given detailed training on the employment of a whole variety of explosives and on how to improvise booby-traps to delay an enemy advance. The training also encompasses the use of mines, although France's position as a signatory to the Ottawa con-

vention, banning the use of landmines, means that the company can no longer train in the deployment of these weapons, only in their clearance. The sniper specialization of the company has, to an extent, grown to encompass the use of all small arms – the Minimi light machine gun is hardly a sniper weapon, but 4th Company was entrusted with carrying out the service trials prior to its adoption.

Legionnaires sent to 4th Company will either receive detailed instruction in the use of explosives or in sniping. The former course involves consider-

Above: A group of legionnaires prepare to embark upon a beach reconnaissance exercise. The Legion is not customarily associated with maritime operations, but maintains a level of expertise within the ranks of 3rd Company of 2 REP to ensure that it has the ability to carry out maritime reconnaissance tasks.

Fire Support

The two main machine guns of the Legion since the 1960s have been the AAT-52 and, more recently, the FN Minimi (known in American service as the M249 squad automatic weapon). The AAT-52 was procured to replace the mixture of French, American, British and even ex-German machine guns used until the end of the Indo-China war. The AAT-52 used the 7.5mm (0.29in) cartridge preferred by the French army to the NATO standard 7.62mm (0.3in), but was a generally reliable weapon. It was rather awkward to carry easily, particularly if fitted with a box to hold the ammunition belt, but served the Legion well for over 40 years; some can still be seen in use today. However, it was clear that for the sort of urban skirmishing common in peacekeeping operations, something newer and easier to use was required.

As a result, the AAT-52 began to be replaced at the end of the 1990s by the 5.56mm (0.22in) FN Minimi, a Belgian-designed weapon. Lighter and easier to handle than the AA 52, the Minimi's cartridge is common to that used in the FAMAS rifle, making the logistics chain easier. The Legion was first seen using the weapon in the Balkans in the mid-1990s, and it is rapidly becoming the standard support weapon for Legion sections.

---

able instruction on the safe handling of explosives and the amount required to carry out certain tasks, and it imbues the legionnaires with the necessary technical understanding to conduct a whole range of demolitions operations.

Snipers, on the other hand, are instructed in the skills of camouflage and concealment, as well as how to shoot over long ranges. Contrary to popular myths, snipers are not necessarily natural shots born with the gift of being able to shoot with phenomenal accuracy – good shooting can be taught. After passing the training course a Legion sniper can engage an enemy target at ranges of over 1km (0.6 miles), with an extremely high expectation of gaining a hit with his first shot. Also, if all has gone well, the sniper firing the shot will remain undetected, relying upon

the concealment skills learned on his training course.

The Legion places a high value on its snipers, since they proved particularly useful in peacekeeping operations in Sarajevo: snipers targeting members of the civilian population succeeded in terrorizing the city's inhabitants, but began to lose enthusiasm when peacekeeping troops started targeting them. The snipers also have an additional 'stay behind' role, which was of more relevance in the Cold War era, when it was assumed that the Warsaw Pact would gain ground on NATO's central front.

In such circumstances, small groups of snipers (along with special forces teams) would not fall back with the main body of NATO troops but would remain in place, behind enemy lines, with the aim of harassing the advancing troops. It

was estimated that a team of snipers could delay an advance by several hours before pulling back to rejoin their lines.

5th Company

The 5th Company was created in 1994 as a maintenance unit rather than as a combat company. 2 REP is the only French infantry regiment to have such a company, as organic maintenance units are normally only to be found within units based overseas or using sophisticated equipment such as tanks. The members of the company are all veterans of combat companies, and have training in a variety of technical fields, such as vehicle maintenance or the repair and care of signals equipment.

As well as ensuring that the regiment's equipment is serviced properly and in a timely fashion, the legionnaires in the company can also be employed as additional infantry to bolster the regimental strength should the need arise. The 5th Company's versatility means that it has been employed in all of the regiment's deployments since 1994.

Perhaps the most important part of 5th Company is the platoon that looks after 2 REP's role-specific equipment – its parachutes. Parachutes are maintained by the *Section de Réparation, d'Entretien et de Pilage de matériels de Parachutage* (Parachute Equipment and Maintenance Platoon; SREPP). The SREPP makes around 16,000 parachute issues per year, and is responsible for the care and preparation of each parachute.

The procedure for this is as follows. First, a parachute will be issued from the store to one of the

Above: Two blue-helmeted legionnaires from 2 REP's 4th Company keep watch over the approaches to a wintry Sarajevo during their deployment to the area in the mid-1990s. The sniper is armed with a Harris M87R 12.7mm (0.50in) sniper rifle, which can engage targets out to a very long range.

members of 2 REP. It will then be used by the paratrooper, recovered, and sent back to SREPP. SREPP then hangs the parachute in a drying tower. It is imperative to ensure that parachutes are completely dry before they are repacked, without the slightest trace of moisture on their fabric, since damp parachutes tend not to work properly. Once dried, the

parachute is inspected for signs of damage. If the parachute or the harness has been damaged in any way, it is sent for repair (or, if too badly damaged, disposed of). The parachute is then folded for repacking. Folding a parachute is not a simple task. If the parachute does not fit into its pack correctly, it may not deploy when next used, so it is essential that every parachute is

folded and packed properly every time. The SREPP has a full-time staff of 21 NCOs and legionnaires, but also trains legionnaires from the five 2 REP combat companies in the arts of parachute maintenance.

It takes two months for the trainees to qualify properly. Five weeks are spent learning how to maintain and fold the parachutes, followed by a month of practical

Above: Legionnaires departing for Saudi Arabia in 1990 check their baggage on the quayside at Toulon. Political disputes within the French government proved to be very frustrating for the legionnaires, who were not certain whether they would participate in the liberation of Kuwait until late in the planning process.

application. In the latter phase, the legionnaires on the 'folding' course prepare parachutes for use by their colleagues, under the watchful eye of the permanent staff of the SREPP.

The first parachute that is prepared for use is then issued to the trainee, who is sent off to carry out a practice jump with it. This step ensures that the trainees pay very careful attention to the instruction that they are given, and reinforces the confidence of all those in 2 REP – they know that the parachute

that they are using has been made ready by someone who would be prepared to jump out of an aircraft with it. Assuming that the trainee has done his job properly and lands safely, he is then deemed to have qualified successfully as a 'folder'.

Qualification is not the end of the training, however, since over the next month and a half, the new 'folder' will work in SREPP preparing more parachutes – although it is essential that such work is done carefully, it needs to be done quite

quickly as well. Over the course of his six weeks with the platoon, the new folder increases the rate at which he prepares parachutes until, by the end of his time, he is expected to be able to fold and pack 27 parachutes in six hours.

Once this hurdle has been negotiated, the legionnaire returns to his company, thus ensuring that each of 2 REP's five companies has a number of specialists in looking after parachutes – something of considerable importance should 2 REP find itself operating away from Calvi and beyond the direct assistance of SREPP.

Scout and Support Company (SSC)

The Scout and Support Company (in French *Compagnie d'Eclairage et d'Appui* – literally Heavy Weapons Support Company) provides the heavy firepower and specialized reconnaissance unit for 2 REP. It consists of six platoons – anti-tank; mortar; reconnaissance; command and the GCP. Prior to restructuring of the French Army, there used to be a second anti-tank platoon and an anti-aircraft platoon equipped with 20mm (0.79in) cannon.

Training for the company largely consists of mastering the heavy weapons to best effect, but the regimental reconnaissance platoon is fully motorized (using P-4 light vehicles) and undergoes additional training on how best to employ vehicles on reconnaissance missions. The members of the company are also given training in camouflage and concealment (a necessary specialization for the role) and in the identification of military equipment from across the world. The vehicles are all equipped with heavy machine guns and anti-tank weapons, so it is necessary for the legionnaires to be proficient in the use of these weapons as well, although these skills are, of course, passed on to the majority of legionnaires as routine training progresses.

The most specialized element of the company, and arguably of the entire 2 REP, is the *Groupe Commando des Parachutistes* (GCP). Every regiment in the *11e Brigade Parachutiste* (to which 2 REP belongs) has a GCP element. The GCP sections, made up of around 30 legionnaires, are not considered to be fully fledged Special Forces (the French Special Forces being the *Commandement des Opérations Spéciales*, or COS), but are trained to carry out difficult missions. The relationship between the GCPs and the COS might be equated (although not exactly) to that between the US Army Rangers and Delta Force, or the Parachute Regiment and the Special Air Service in Britain. The GCP units

Above: Legionnaires observe NATO helicopters flying past as they patrol in Kosovo, 1999. They are aboard a VAB armoured reconnaissance vehicle, used to provide rapid mobility and a degree of protection while on patrol duties.

Above: A patrol stops for a break during a Legion deployment to Chad in the 1980s. The legionnaires spent a great deal of time on patrol, attempting to prevent Libyan-backed rebels from entering the southern part of the country, which was under government control. The occasional encounters with the rebels proved to be notably costly to the enemy.

are *11e Brigade Parachutiste*'s rapid reaction units, on short notice to deploy.

The main role of the GCP is reconnaissance through air insertion, using HALO (High Altitude, Low Opening) or HAHO (High Altitude, High Opening) techniques. As the names suggest, HALO drops involve leaving the transport aircraft at high altitude and opening the parachute canopy after falling several thousand feet. By contrast, in HAHO drops the canopy is opened shortly after leaving the aircraft.

HALO insertions are designed to minimize the risk of visual or aural detection by the enemy, since it is extremely difficult to see a parachutist falling at near terminal velocity without their canopy deployed and impossible to hear from the ground an aircraft flying at 9100m (30,000ft).

The HAHO insertion is also intended to reduce the risk of detection, and by using steerable parachutes the HAHO jumper can leave the transport aircraft and glide a considerable distance to his objective. To achieve the necessary pre-

cision, HAHO parachutists are often equipped with a small Global Positioning System (GPS) device to allow them to navigate to their landing zone. The advantage of a HAHO assault is that the transport aircraft does not need to enter hostile airspace. This in turn means that while the transport may be detected on enemy radar screens, the opposition does not regard an aircraft flying some distance outside its borders as representing a threat.

The transport is likely to be flying at an altitude that means it is impossible to distinguish from a civilian airliner, while the radar signature presented by a small group of paratroopers leaving the aircraft and then gliding in towards their target is miniscule.

Naturally enough, the need to conduct HALO and HAHO operations means that additional, specialized parachute training is carried out. The members of the GCP are all experienced legionnaires, and recently arrived men will not be considered for the group. This is understandable when the array of possible GCP missions is appreciated. As well as the special parachute techniques noted above, the GCP members are expected to be able to carry out insertion by boat (working with 3rd Company) or by submarine. The GCP have also carried out operations to track down war criminals and have an anti-terrorism role, for which training in hostage rescue is undertaken. Although the 11th Brigade's GCPs are not necessarily the lead element in anti-terrorism operations (this being the purview of the Gendarmerie's *Groupement d'Intervention de la Gendarmerie Nationale*, or GIGN), it is quite possible that a GCP force might be employed in a situation where time was of the essence, or deploying GIGN was not an option.

As well as being proficient in the skills of 1st, 2nd and 3rd Companies, members of the GCP must also have one of the core skills of 4th Company, and are expected to have completed the Desert and Jungle training courses as well. This means that the GCP soldiers are amongst the best trained in the world, and are able to make a major contribution to the success of the Legion or 11th Brigade as a whole.

Commando Training

All legionnaires can volunteer for Commando training, and those posted to 1st Company, 2 REP often find themselves sent on this course, which is carried out at the Mont Louis Commando Training Centre in the Pyrenees. The course provides training in a variety of specializations, including abseiling and climbing techniques, explosives training, hand-to-hand combat and instruction on amphibious operations. Once the training in these fields has been completed, the legionnaire puts it into practice in a mock raiding operation. The commando course produces legionnaires who are able to contribute to all the companies of 2 REP, and who have considerable utility for the infantry and engineering regiments.

Rescue at Djibouti

On 3 February 1976, a school bus carrying the children of French servicemen was hijacked in Djibouti by terrorists demanding the release of prisoners held there. The French anti-terrorist unit, the *Groupement d'Intervention de la Gendarmerie Nationale* (GIGN) was sent to Djibouti to plan a rescue mission. It was clear that the open ground around the bus would make a covert approach by an assault team very difficult, so the commander of GIGN, Lieutenant Prouteau, decided that should the bus need to be stormed, snipers would be used to kill the terrorists at long range, with a rescue party standing by to rush to the bus and recover the children. A further complicating factor was that the bus was being held on the coastal road between Djibouti and Somalia, and it became clear that the Somali authorities had aided the terrorists. As a result, members of 2 REP were deployed to provide support to GIGN.

Food laced with tranquilizers was sent out to the bus, and the children duly fell asleep, and as they slumped in their seats, their silhouettes disappeared from sight. Finally, the GIGN sniper teams were able to engage all five terrorists in the vicinity of the bus at once. They opened fire, and killed four gunmen who were inside the vehicle, and another just outside. Before the GIGN team could rush to remove the children, a Somali border post opened fire, pinning them down.

At this point, 2 REP opened fire on the border post. The legionnaires poured a huge volume of fire into Somali positions and suppressed them; however, a sixth terrorist was able to make it to the bus under the cover of the Somali fire. Prouteau and two of his men disregarded the incoming fire and ran to intercept the sixth terrorist. The terrorist managed to kill one small girl, but was killed by the three GIGN men before he could harm any more. 2 REP then mopped up the remaining Somali resistance, and having secured the area, the surviving 29 children were evacuated.

Terrain-Specific Training

The training programmes outlined above do not only apply to 2 REP (and this is true of parachuting as well); they can be found throughout the Legion. In addition, some specific environmental training is given to those units deployed in desert or jungle conditions. The Legion is fortunate to have overseas facilities that allow training to be carried out in these environments.

For the desert course, carried out at the Legion's base in Djibouti, legionnaires learn survival basics, such as ensuring that the correct amount of water is consumed each day, and more complicated issues such as the proper use of weapons in a desert environment. Range finding can be more difficult given heat haze and wind-blown sand, desert navigation must be mastered, and knowledge of the wild variations in climate is imparted: while the desert may be baking hot during the day, it can be incredibly cold at night. Furthermore, the notion that all deserts are unyielding oceans of sand under a baking sun is completely misleading. Some desert is more akin to scrubland, with low-lying vegetation and rocky terrain, while the weather can vary from scorching sunshine through sandstorms to heavy rain.

When the Legion fought in the Gulf War of 1991, the weather conditions in the Kuwaiti Theatre of Operations were the worst in the region for 40 years, and included torrential rain and freezing conditions. The Legion, by virtue of its long experience in Algeria and Morocco, has learned much about desert warfare, and its course builds extensively upon this long-held knowledge.

The jungle training course is carried out in French Guiana at the base of *3e Régiment Etranger d'Infanterie* (3rd Legion Infantry Regiment; 3 REI). Like the desert training course, legionnaires are given instruction in how to survive in the unique terrain presented by jungle. This training includes information about plants that are safe to eat in an emergency (and those that

Above: Three legionnaires move through a water course while at the jungle training centre in Guiana. They are practising a stealthy approach on a target, with the use of the river as a means of gaining a degree of surprise.

are not), and gives an introduction to some of the dangerous wildlife that can be found in jungles.

For example, the legionnaires are taught snake identification, enabling them to distinguish the most venomous creatures from those that do not represent a threat. They are also put in close proximity to snakes to build confidence, and taught how to avoid antagonizing a snake; in many instances the snake will be as nervous as the legionnaire, and simply standing still and not appearing to be a threat will be enough to prevent the snake from attacking. Some of the more aggressive snakes are more of a problem, and for these creatures a combat shotgun is often the easiest solution. However, the hazard here is that the use of the shotgun may compromise the location of a patrol.

As well as the complications offered by snakes, poisonous insects are another jungle problem. The legionnaires learn basic anti-insect precautions, such as making sure that boots are checked for the presence of jungle creatures before putting them on and not sleeping on the jungle floor. In addition to these basics, the skills needed for jungle fighting are delivered. Jungle fighting demands careful movement, as the slightest sound may give away a position.

Ambush and counter-ambush are the mainstays of jungle fighting techniques. Legionnaires are taught how to initiate a jungle ambush, and, equally importantly, how to break contact with the enemy should the need arise. Given the nature of the jungle, breaking contact must be done carefully to avoid splitting a patrol

Above: A legionnaire makes a grab for the hand of a colleague standing on the bank as he carries out amphibious training at the legion base near Marseilles. As can be seen from the strain on his face, this training is as rigorous as any other conducted by the Legion, even though it is not a skill commonly used by any legionnaires other than those in 3rd Company of 2 REP.

up, and is rather less simple than might be assumed.

The Versatile Legion

The specialist training carried out by legionnaires equips them for a variety of situations that they might encounter when deployed on operations. This is, of course, true of all military formations, but the Legion is notable for the fact that a considerable array of differing expertise can be found throughout whichever Legion unit is deployed.

Some members of the infantry regiments will be experts in reconnaissance, or the use of support weapons, or be commando trained.

The same may apply to members of the cavalry regiment, which is, of course, fully competent in the art of armoured reconnaissance missions. One of the hallmarks of the Legion is its versatility, and the accessibility of specialist training means that such versatility is spread throughout its ranks.

The Legion is a particularly effective formation, well suited to the demands of modern conflict, where the skills required to fight in urban terrain, carry out covert surveillance, to use armoured vehicles and build bridges and infrastructure may all be needed in the same deployment.

Uniform and Equipment

With a history dating back to 1831, the Legion has made use of a great variety of weapons and vehicles during its existence. Like all other French units, it has suffered periods when the equipment available to it was not adequate for the task in hand, often because of a lack of government willingness to procure the most up-to-date firearms or technologies.

It is often easy to overlook the fact that the Legion was, until relatively recently, a fully professionalized element of the French Army, unlike other formations that employed conscripts. Although the French have now moved away from conscription, the Legion still retains its reputation as a 'professional' component of the French armed forces.

However, despite this special reputation, the Legion has always largely been equipped with standard French Army equipment. The versatile nature of the unit means that it has often employed a greater range of this equipment than others, but there are few items found in the Legion's inventory that cannot be found in use with other

Above: Legionnaires wearing full chemical and biological warfare protection equipment practice operating in the hot and uncomfortable protective suits. In the intense desert heat, the wearing of such suits rapidly reduces the effectiveness of troops, although this can be offset to a small degree by acclimatisation through wearing them in training, as seen here.

Above: Parading legionnaires provide a close-up of the unique FAMAS assault rifle. As they are being used for drill, these rifles are not fitted with the 25-round magazine that is standard. The folding bipod can be seen along the top of the weapon, just beneath the elongated carrying handle that contains the rifle's sights.

French Army formations. In recent years, some parts of the Legion have begun to make use of items, particularly weapons, that are not regularly found in the French Army at large, but these usually remain confined to the more specialized parts of the Legion, rather than being on general issue.

Legion Uniform

The basic Legion uniform of today is the *Centre Europe F2* (Central European F2) camouflage uniform. The pattern was introduced in 1991, and consists of four colours – tan, brown , green and black. The initial issue of the uniform had lower pockets on the jacket, while the F2 pattern does not. The move to camouflage uniform throughout the French Army owes something to the Legion's history: a camouflage pattern uniform was issued in the aftermath of World War II, but withdrawn from use in 1963. The reason for this was that the uniform was felt to be a reminder of the mutinous 1 REP.

The all-green M1947 pattern was replaced in 1971 by M1964 'satin 300' pattern fatigues, and these remained in use for the next 25 years. They were still common apparel for the Legion in 1991, but the deployment of troops to the Gulf in 1991 led to the creation of new desert camouflage. The camouflage pattern consisted of three colours: tan, light green and brown, and the design was adapted for the Central European pattern. This meant that unlike the British and American armies (to name but two), the French standard temperate uniform evolved from a desert pattern, rather than the other way around.

In addition to the basic uniform, legionnaires usually wear a green beret with silver Legion badge over

The White Képi (*Képi Blanc*)

Along with the red (actually maroon) beret of the British Parachute Regiment and the US Army Special Operations Forces' green beret, the white képi of the Foreign Legion is one of the most famous items of military headgear in the world.

Although the white képi is the most famous item of Legion uniform, the Legion had been established for over 100 years before it became officially recognised headgear. Originally, it was the képi's cover that was white, rather than the képi itself. The cover was designed to protect the wearer from the sun, and often came with a neck flap to provide additional defence against sun-stroke. Other French army units had a similar head cover, and it was not worn year-round.

After some 70 years in which the képi worn by the Legion was identical to that worn by other French army units, a change occurred – but by accident, and over time. In 1907, the colour of the képi cover was changed to khaki (again for all units). However, the fact that the Legion was permanently based in the desert meant that the sun bleached the khaki white; coupled with regular washing, the Legion found itself with a distinctive képi once again. There was a problem, however, since the white képi stood out, and made legionnaires a target for enemy snipers. This prompted orders that the cover be dyed – the favoured method was to soak it in coffee grounds. However, further exposure to the sun and washing returned the colour to white again. It should also be noted that the Legion did not wear the white képi all year round, since during the winter, the cover was removed to show the usual képi colours of red with a blue band.

Although the most recognizable symbol of the Legion, officers and non-commissioned officers do not usually wear the white képi, instead wearing one in midnight blue with a red top edge. At the top of the body, lines of braid in either gold or silver denote rank, correlating with the number of lines on the shoulder boards. A further unusual feature of the képi is the chin strap (gold for officers and warrant officers and black for other ranks) that circles the base of the képi and which lies on the peak: it is, in fact, false. Should a chin strap be required, a second one of the appropriate colour is attached. However, there is photographic evidence that shows officers in Indo-China wearing the képi cover, with holes cut into the fabric so that their rank symbols are showing.

the right eye as their headgear. An alternative headgear is the famed *képi blanc*. In combat, the Spectra ballistic helmet is usually worn. This has largely replaced the M1978 helmet, and is notable for the way in which it 'bulges' above the wearer's ears – the design allows ear defenders or communications headsets to be worn beneath the helmet. As additional protection, legionnaires are now equipped with body armour. The body armour is fitted with integral straps and D-rings to allow direct attachment of personal equipment. In addition to a working uniform, the legionnaire will also have a parade dress. Made in a grey khaki shade known as '*terre de France*', this smart uniform is worn on ceremonial occasions (complete with large red epaulettes that replace the shoulder rank boards for such events) and when the legionnaire is 'walking out'.

Handguns

For reasons that are not altogether clear, the French armament industry has never had a great reputation for producing handguns in the way that Italian and American arms manufacturers (to name but two) have secured. Although the utility of the handgun for military operations has been the subject of much doubt and debate over the years, there is little denying that such firearms are useful secondary weapons. They are an acceptable alternative to a rifle in close-quarter combat, where the length of the primary weapon may make handling it awkward and the relative lack of stopping power of the pistol at ranges over 20m (65ft) is not problematic.

8mm Lebel Modèle 1892 Revolver

The need to replace the French Army's stock of 1870s vintage black-powder pistols led to the introduction of a more modern weapon in the form of a revolver known to the troops as the Lebel, but known officially as the *Pistol Revolver Modèle 1892* or the *Modèle d'Ordnance*. The revolver was the first made in Europe to incorporate a swing-out cylinder, rather than use the laborious gate-loading mechanism or a break-open style. The cylinder swung out to the right, which was not as convenient for right-handed users as the more common left-hand opening weapons that followed, and spent cases were ejected using a central hand-operated rod under the barrel.

The Lebel fired a special 8mm (0.31in) cartridge using a double-action trigger mechanism, which was heavy and made accurate shooting at any distance difficult. The main drawback of the gun was that the cartridge was badly underpowered and even at short ranges inflicted wounds that were usually insufficient to stop an opponent unless the bullet hit a vital

spot. Nonetheless, the Lebel was a popular weapon, since soldiers who used it valued its reliability above all other features.

As the French munitions industry did not have notable success in designing a replacement weapon during the inter-war period, the Lebel saw some use in World War II, finally leaving French service when reliable semi-automatic pistols were available in sufficient numbers.

7.65mm Pistole Automatique Modèle 1935A/1935S

Although the automatic (self-loading) pistol gained favour in the early part of the twentieth century, the French arms industry was slow to develop a service weapon of this sort. A variety of Spanish-made weapons were procured as an interim measure before the Model 1935 was introduced. The design was based upon that of the famed Colt M1911A1 pistol, although the visual similarities between the two guns are superficial at best.

The French also chose a different calibre for the Model 1935, in the form of the 7.65mm (0.30in) Long cartridge. This was a most

---

The Long Service Stripe

All NCOs and legionnaires who have completed their first five-year contract and who have re-enlisted will wear a single inverted chevron below the left arm badge. They receive a second after completing ten years of service, and yet another upon completion of 15 years. Legionnaires are not supposed to complete more than 20 years' service, but there is photographic evidence of one senior NCO from 1979 wearing no fewer than *five* chevrons, denoting more than 30 years in the Legion. There could be little doubt that he had served for this length of time, since he was seen wearing World War II campaign medals – which meant a minimum of 34 years with the Legion, and probably a little longer.

unusual calibre, little used outside France.

The Model 1935A was replaced in production by the Model 1935S, which was a variant developed to make the weapon easier to mass produce, an important consideration as the 1930s saw Europe head towards another war. The 1935S had a straighter butt, and the barrel protruded from the weapon at the muzzle end, whereas it was enclosed on the 1935A. Both guns had a magazine that held eight rounds of ammunition.

The two Model 1935 pistols were perfectly serviceable weapons, and the Germans were sufficiently impressed with the weapon to take it into use when stocks became available to them after the fall of France. The Free French forces used the Model 1935 as well, and the gun remained in service for some time after World War II, especially in colonial garrisons. This meant that the Legion made considerable use of the Model 1935 until later handguns appeared to replace it.

Above: Suspected Viet Minh guerrillas are questioned by members of a Legion patrol. The oppressive heat encountered in the Tonkin valley can be judged from the lack of a shirt on the man carrying out the questioning. He is armed with a self-loading pistol, most probably a Model 1935A.

Right: The Model 1935A 9mm (0.35in) pistol saw service with the Legion between its introduction prior to World War II and its withdrawal from wide-spread use some 20 years later. The Model 1935 was another in a range of solid and serviceable French handguns that did not gain much attention outside their country of origin.

9mm MAS Modèle 1950

The MAS Model 1950 originated with the need after World War II for new weapons to equip the French forces. It was a perfectly competent design that did not win any great plaudits, but which met the essential requirement of any military weapon – namely that the user could pull the trigger with consider-able confidence that the gun would fire as intended. Based on this, the French Army was more than happy to obtain the weapon in large numbers, and it remained in pro-duction for 20 years, and in use for 30, eventually being superseded by the later MAB PA15.

The Model 1950 carried nine rounds of ammunition in its maga-zine, which was a perfectly respectable figure for its time; the move towards large-capacity pistols had not begun when the gun was designed (the Browning GP35 was the only weapon in wide-spread service at that time with a magazine holding more than 10 rounds).

9mm MAB PA15

The PA15 began life as a weapon designed for civilian use, but it attracted the attention of the French Army, which was searching for a new handgun to replace the oldest of its stocks of Model 1950s. As with its predecessor, the PA15 is not

a well-known weapon, since it is only in large-scale use with the French Army, and has not been widely exported. The most notable feature of the pistol is its capacious 15-round magazine, which means that the gun has a bulky handgrip that is perhaps a little wide for those with smaller hands.

The French Army began to take deliveries of the PA15 in 1975, pro-duction continued until the late 1980s, and it was another decade before a replacement was consid-ered. Again, as the standard French service weapon, it was inevitable that the Legion would make wide-spread use of the PA15, which was first used in action at Kolwezi in 1978.

Submachine Guns

Developed during World War I, the submachine gun was intended to provide troops with a handy auto-matic weapon for close-quarter combat, as opposed to the overly long, bolt-action rifles with which they were normally equipped. Few submachine guns were issued in the war, and they only really began

to gain acceptance in military circles in the late 1920s. To make the weapons controllable, the sub-machine guns all employed pistol-calibre cartridges, a feature that remains to this day. One problem associated with this choice was the fact that such rounds are not partic-ularly effective over long ranges. During the 1970s the submachine gun fell from favour as a frontline weapon once small-calibre assault rifles, which offered controllable automatic fire in conjunction with better long-range shooting charac-teristics, began to make their pres-ence felt. However, the submachine gun is not dead as a concept, remaining popular as a personal defence weapon and for use in close-quarter fighting.

7.65mm MAS Modèle 1938

The MAS Model 1938 (usually known simply as the MAS 38) resulted from a long period of development just prior to the out-break of World War II. It was a sophisticated weapon for its time, using a complicated firing mecha-nism with a bolt travel employing a

Below: Legionnaires engage the Viet Minh from a fire trench. The old-style helmets worn by the men at the left and right are noticeable in this photograph, another demonstration of the lack of up to date equipment in the French armed forces after World War II. The man on the right is using an MAS 36 rifle with a rifle grenade attached to the barrel.

very long return spring. To keep the gun compact, much of this mechanism was accommodated in the butt, which made manufacturing more difficult than it might have been.

The MAS 38 also had a flap that covered the magazine housing when the magazine was withdrawn

from the gun, to prevent dirt entering the mechanism. While this was a sensible idea, it was another complication – most other submachine guns managed to operate perfectly well without this feature. Despite the high standard of manufacture, the French Army rejected the gun, but changed its mind when it was

obvious that war with Germany was probable, and as many weapons as possible would need to be procured. The MAS 38 was used by Vichy French forces, and remained in production during the war. Many weapons went to Indo-China, and the weapon was commonly employed by Legionnaires there in the early stages of the conflict.

A good gun, hampered by the unusual 7.65mm (0.30in) long round and its slow production rate (the result of the weapon's complexities), the MAS 38 did not receive the recognition that it deserved, and faded from use.

9mm Sten Gun

The Sten Gun was one of the crudest weapons ever produced, but the low quality was in many ways intentional. After the British Expeditionary Force had withdrawn from France in 1940, it was necessary for the British Army to restock with weapons, particularly submachine guns. With the threat of imminent German invasion, the requirement was for a 9mm (0.35in) weapon that was simple, and which could be mass produced.

The Sten met these criteria admirably. Made from pressings, sheet steel and metal tubing, a Sten Gun could be assembled for as little as 37 pence (US$2 at the time). Despite being crude, it was effective, although the magazine was to prove problematic throughout the gun's life, even in the slightly more sophisticated versions that appeared from 1944 (and which remained in British service until the 1950s). The magazine, which held 32 rounds, was prone to damage to the feed lips, resulting in jams.

9mm PAMAS G1

For perhaps the first time, the French Army is equipped with a handgun that is well-known, in the form of the PAMAS G1. This is a licence-produced version of the Italian Beretta Model 92. Instead of buying an indigenous weapon to replace the PA15, the French Army's decision to adopt the PAMAS was influenced by the fact that the Gendarmerie had decided to procure the weapon when it was searching for a new pistol. The Gendarmerie took the PAMAS into service in 1989, with the army following shortly afterwards. The PAMAS began to be seen more frequently in the 1990s, most notably on peacekeeping deployments to the former Yugoslavia, a task with which the Legion was heavily involved. Although the PAMAS is a well-regarded pistol, some commentators have expressed doubts about the reliability of the pistol in the most arduous combat conditions – the US Army M9 pistol is another version of the Beretta M92, and after-action reports from Afghanistan have been less than complimentary about the pistol's serviceability.

These feeding problems were a major cause of irritation, as was the weapon's habit of going off if dropped, even with the safety catch on. The Sten was parachuted to French resistance groups and issued on a large scale to Free French forces. By this means, 13e Demi-Brigade de Légion Etrangère (13th Legion Demi-Brigade; 13 DBLE) came into possession of the weapon, and more were provided after the war.

The Legion made use of the Sten in Indo-China, but – as was the case with the British Army – legionnaires who could find an alternative in the shape of the American Thompson submachine gun (the original 'Tommy Gun') did so.

0.45in M1 Thompson

Firing the 11mm (0.45in) Colt pistol round, the Thompson was one of the classic early submachine gun designs, with its origins in World War I when the US Army required

such a weapon for trench fighting. As it was, the war ended before the Thompson entered service, and it became better known as the weapon of choice for American gangsters during the Prohibition era. The US Army finally began to purchase the Thompson in 1928. As World War II approached, both Britain and France placed orders for large numbers of the Thompson. These had not arrived by the time of France's surrender in 1940, and the weapons all went to Britain.

Two types of Thompson were sent to the United Kingdom – the M1928 model with a forward pistol grip for the non-firing hand, and the slightly simpler M1928A1, which had a horizontal foregrip beneath the barrel instead of the pistol grip of the earlier model.

The drum magazines holding 50 or 100 rounds proved troublesome and were replaced by a simple vertical box holding 20 or 30 rounds. An even simpler version, the M1, was produced when the United States Army placed huge orders for more of the weapon, and while the M1928A1 and M1 looked very similar, there were significant differences between the two (aimed at simplifying the manufacturing process). The Free French forces were provided with large numbers of Thompsons towards the end of the war, and a number were passed on to the Legion, which made good use of them in Indo-China.

The Thompson faded from use in the French forces as the indigenously-made MAT 49 entered service, but a few may still be encountered in unlikely places around the world: one US police department still held stocks of the gun as late as the 1980s, 60 years after the first Thompson had been produced.

9mm MAT 49

By 1949, French military authorities noted that there were increasing logistical problems resulting from the use of three different calibres for the army's submachine guns, so it was decided to standardize upon the 9mm (0.35in) Parabellum round. A design from the *Manufacture d'Armes de Tulle* (hence the MAT) was chosen to replace the MAS 38, Sten and Thompson, and entered production in 1949 (hence the 49 in the designation). The MAT was made from

Right: Three legionnaires take a break from patrolling. They are all carrying MAT 49 submachine guns, a versatile weapon that saw over 30 years service with the French Army. The man in the centre has folded the magazine housing so that it is lying horizontally beneath the barrel and is thus easier to carry.

Above: A member of 2 REP covers a colleague with a Heckler & Koch MP5 SD6 suppressed submachine gun. The reduced firing report of the SD series of MP5s makes them extremely useful weapons for covert operations, and they are widely used by specialist forces alongside the standard model MP5s. The weapon is not widely issued in the Legion, with the FAMAS being the standard personal weapon for all legionnaires. The MP5 is commonly held to be the best submachine gun available today.

heavy-gauge steel stampings, which made it an impressively robust weapon, but without being too heavy. Another notable design feature was the magazine housing, which as well as serving as the forward hand grip, could fold forward (with the magazine still in it) to reduce the overall bulk of the weapon during transportation. A catch was depressed and the whole housing was folded forward; returning the magazine to the vertical position for firing was equally simple. When the magazine was in the forward position, a flap moved into place to cover the space left, thus preventing dirt from entering the weapon. To keep the weapon compact when travelling, a simple sliding stock was attached to the gun; when slid forward, it almost halved the weapon's length.

All of these features made the MAT 49 extremely reliable, even in the most arduous conditions, and it was very popular, particularly with the paratroops of *1er* and *2e Régiment Etranger de Parachutistes* (1st and 2nd Legion

Parachute Regiments; 1 and 2 REP). The last notable use of the MAT 49 by the Legion came at Kolwezi in 1978, shortly before the gun was replaced by the FAMAS assault rifle. Although the MAT 49 is no longer employed by the French Army, it was produced in sufficient numbers and exported widely enough to ensure that it can still be encountered in various parts of the world.

Heckler & Koch MP5

After the MAT 49 was retired from service, the French Army was equipped not with a mixture of rifles and submachine guns, but just the FAMAS rifle. However, the utility of submachine guns in certain situations meant that more specialized units in the French armed forces looked for a replacement. The choice was relatively simple, since the MP5 was (and probably still is) the best weapon of its type available. The weapon entered production in the 1960s, and was relatively little known outside West Germany (as it then was) until the late 1970s, when the German counter-terrorist unit GSG9 employed them in the hostage rescue at Mogadishu.

The weapon became even more famous in 1980, when the British Special Air Service (SAS) stormed the Iranian embassy in London to free 20 people held by terrorists. Since that action, the MP5 has become a familiar sight. Almost every major special forces unit in the West uses the MP5, employing several of the different versions that are available.

As well as the standard weapon, a 'silenced' version (actually suppressed rather than silent, since there is some noise when the gun is fired) is available and widely used. The Legion *Groupe Commando des Parachutistes* (GCPs) are particularly fond of the silenced MP5, and tend to be the main users of the weapon. Although the GCPs are not the primary French anti-terrorist unit, they are trained to conduct hostage rescues, and the MP5 is almost always used as the weapon of choice in such scenarios.

Rifles

As might be imagined, the Legion has used a good number of rifles since it was created in 1831. The section below looks at some of the most prominent ones from the later part of the nineteenth century onwards. It should be noted that there were several service rifles in use in the late 1800s and early 1900s, with standardization on one particular rifle type not taking place (incredibly) until after World War II. Although the need for a standardized rifle was appreciated, it was not possible to arm every French soldier with the same weapon as a result of funding difficulties and the practical reason that cavalrymen required a shorter rifle than infantrymen. Not all of the rifles used by the Legion are mentioned here, merely those that are most notable.

11mm Fusil Gras Modèle 1874

The Model 1874 rifle was perhaps most significant for being the first French service rifle to employ a metal cartridge case. A single-shot weapon, it fired a large 11mm (0.43in) round. Single-shot weapons began to become obsolete with the widespread appear-

ance of magazine rifles, although the Model 1874 remained a key weapon for many years, albeit in the hands of colonial and second-line troops.

The last Model 1874s were finally removed from French service during the course of World War II. It was certainly the oldest rifle in use in 1939 amongst any of the combatants. The Legion employed the Model 1874 for rather less time, using it until the late 1880s when the new Lebel rifle entered service.

8mm Fusil Lebel Modèle 1886

By the early 1880s, the French army took the decision to use a smaller-calibre rifle round, selecting one with a calibre of 8mm (0.31in). A new rifle was required, and the Model 1886 was the result. The weapon was commonly known as the 'Lebel' after the officer who led the study commission that recommended the adoption of the 8mm round.

Apart from the change in calibre, the new weapon was not a major advance on the Gras Model 1874, employing exactly the same bolt action. The Lebel did carry more ammunition, having a tubular eight-round magazine underneath the barrel.

Although this represented a considerable improvement over the single-shot Gras, the tubular magazine placed the bullets nose-to-tail, which meant that there was a risk that a sudden impact might cause the nose of a round to hit the primer of the cartridge in front, thus setting off a deeply undesirable chain reaction. Despite these disadvantages, it was a pleasant weapon to handle, and it was generally popular. As standard issue within the French services, it was employed by the Legion as a matter of course.

Like the Gras 1874, the Lebel enjoyed a long service career, with the last of the weapons being withdrawn during the course of World War II.

8mm Fusil Berthier Modèle 1907

It was not long before the disadvantages of some of the design features of the Lebel rifle began to be appreciated by the French Army, and this prompted a decision to build an improved rifle. Since the Lebel was in large-scale production, the process of introducing the

new rifle took a great deal of time, and it was not until 1907 that it was completed with the introduction of the Berthier.

The first Berthiers were carbines, and employed by the cavalry from 1890, with the full-length weapons taking rather more time to reach the troops. The Model 1907 was

intended only for use in the colonies, which meant that the Legion was amongst the first units to take the weapon on charge; the outbreak of World War I meant that the idea of limiting the weapon to overseas service was abandoned, and the Berthier was widely used during the conflict.

Left: Men of 13 DBLE parade in Saigon in 1947. They are carrying MAS 36 bolt-action rifles, the standard rifle of the French Army. The MAS 36 was a sound weapon, but overly complicated. It was replaced by the MAS 49, a similar looking but rather better semi-automatic rifle.

Although the Berthier was a popular rifle, it suffered in comparison with the Lebel by having only three 8mm (0.31in) rounds in its magazine. This deficiency led to an alteration to the basic design, resulting in the Model 1916 which was virtually identical to the Model 1907, but had five rounds. To ease loading, the rounds could be inserted into the magazine using a charging clip, obviating the need to load them one at a time, as had been the case with the Model 1907.

7.5mm Fusil MAS 36

In 1924, the French Army decided to adopt a new 7.5mm (0.29in) round for its rifles, leading to the conversion of some of the earlier weapons to accommodate the new calibre. However, the opportunity to replace the old designs with a completely new weapon was taken, and this ultimately led to the introduction of the MAS 36. This was a modified Mauser-style bolt-action weapon, with a magazine of five rounds. For some reason, the decision was taken to alter the Mauser action so that the locking lugs on the bolt were at the back of the rifle's receiver rather than on the bolt head.

The result was that the bolt handle was at a rather awkward angle. In common with most French weapons up to this point, the MAS 36 was not fitted with a safety catch.

The MAS 36 was not a particularly outstanding weapon, but did its job well enough. Unfortunately for the French Army, issue was slow, and not all frontline units were equipped with the rifle when war broke out. The Free French forces thought well enough of the MAS 36 to retain it as their preferred weapon, although logistical demands meant that British and American weapons tended to predominate as time went on. At the end of the war, the MAS 36 was placed back into production, and large numbers were used for some years. The Legion made good use of the weapon in North Africa and Indo-China, and many were retained as ceremonial weapons.

These can still be seen today, although not in the hands of the majority of the marching troops. Instead, the unit flag is attached to a ramrod inserted into the barrel of the weapon, and the MAS 36 is now literally used as a flagpole when the unit colour is being marched around.

.303in Rifle No.4 Mark 1 (Lee Enfield)

Derived from the Short Magazine Lee Enfield (SMLE) that had gained fame in World War I, the No.4 rifle differed mainly in being easier to manufacture, having some alterations to the sights and, most notably, by the deletion of the SMLE's nose cap, which altered the appearance of the weapon. The No.4 (and the SMLE) had a magazine containing 10 rounds of 7.7mm (.303in) ammunition, giving it the highest ammunition capacity of any bolt-action rifle employed in either world war. The Legion came by a large number via the Free

Above: A legionnaire machine-gunner rests his M1924/49 machine gun on the barrel of his colleague's rifle as they pause to observe the ground ahead of them. Although an old design, the M1924 was a highly regarded weapon that saw service until the 1960s.

French forces, and took a significant number to Algeria and Indo-China after the war. Alongside the MAS 36 and the American supplied M1 Garand and M1 Carbine, the No.4 was a stop-gap until the indigenous semi-automatic MAS 49 rifle was introduced to standardize the number of rifle calibres in use in the French Army. Although a stop-gap, the No.4 could not be regarded as being in any way inferior to its contemporaries; indeed, many experts rate the Lee Enfield series of weapons to be the finest bolt-action battle rifles ever produced.

Rifle, Caliber .30, Model 1903

Commonly known as the 'Springfield' the Model 1903 was an excellent service weapon that was familiar to the French through its use by the US Army in World War I. A very accurate weapon, it was the standard American sniper rifle throughout World War II, and was still used in this role as late as the 1950s.

Although most American units employed the M1 Garand during WWII, the Springfield was also employed on a large scale. The

Carbine, Caliber .30 M1/M1A1/M2

Designed as a weapon for second-line troops, the M1 Carbine was an extremely popular weapon because of its light weight and pleasant handling characteristics. By the end of WWII, over six million had been built. Fitted with a 15- or 30-round box magazine, the M1's major drawback was the round that it fired – an intermediate-power cartridge that lacked power, even at close ranges.

This did not prove a deterrent to many users, who were prepared to accept this problem in return for the handiness offered by the gun. The M1A1 was fitted with a folding stock so that it could be used by airborne units, and this was followed by the M2, which could fire in full-automatic mode.

The Legion, and particularly its parachute battalions, were enthused by the M1 and its derivatives, and put the weapon to good use in Indo-China and Algeria.

Replacement by the MAS 49 followed in due course, but the Legion retained many of its carbines for longer than other units; the weapon was still being used in Algeria in 1959.

Legion came by its rifles in the same way in which it procured other foreign service rifles, namely through these weapons being given to the Free French forces. As with these other rifles, the Springfield remained in service until replaced by the MAS 49 in the course of the 1950s.

Rifle, Caliber .30 M1 (Garand)

The Garand was the first self-loading rifle to be accepted for military service, when the US Army adopted it in 1932. Some 5,500,000 Garands were produced during the war, and a proportion of these weapons were provided to the Free French forces. When the war ended, many Garands went to the Legion, and they feature in many photographs of legionnaires taken in Indo-China.

An accurate and hard-hitting weapon, the Garand was popular with those who used it. The US Army replaced the Garand with the M14, which was essentially a Garand in 7.62mm (0.30in) NATO calibre and with a 20-round box magazine replacing the Garand's eight-round clip.

7.5mm Fusil Mitrailleur Modèle 49

The MAS 36 was the last new-design, bolt-action rifle to enter service with any major army, while its successor was one of the first semi-automatic rifles to be taken on charge. The *Fusil Mitrailleur Modèle 49* (MAS 49) resembled the MAS 36, but was in fact a completely new design As the number in the designation suggests, it was introduced in 1949 as a replacement for the wide variety of weapons in use by the French Army at the time, which ranged from British and American weapons supplied in World War II

to some pre-war French weapons. The Legion was amongst the first units to be given the weapon, and it proved its worth in Algeria and Indo-China.

The MAS 49 underwent modifications in 1956 to produce the MAS 49/56, which remained in service with the French Army until the mid-1980s as re-equipment with the FAMAS took place. Although a few weapons were modified to accept the then-standard NATO calibre of 7.62 x 51mm (0.30 x 2in), the French insisted on using their own 7.5mm (0.29in) round.

A robust and effective weapon, the MAS 49 served the French Army and the Legion well, with the Legion's last operational uses of the gun coming at Kolwezi in 1978 and in Chad. An effective and popular weapon, the MAS 49 was slightly hindered by having just 10 rounds in the magazine, which was something of an anachronism by the time that it was retired – standard service rifles in other countries invariably had 20- or 30-round magazines instead.

5.56mm SIG SG540

When the time came to consider replacing the MAS 49, the French Army decided to move to a 5.56mm (0.22in) weapon, and settled upon the FAMAS. While FAMAS production was gearing up, the army procured a licence-built rifle in the form of the SG540. This was a weapon of Swiss design, produced in France by Manhurin.

As common with all Swiss rifles, the SG540 was a magnificent rifle, built to the highest standards (and, as a result, rather more expensive than its contemporaries). It came with a number of features designed to make it user-friendly, including a folding butt and a trigger guard that could be folded to allow the weapon to be fired more easily by someone wearing heavy arctic mittens. The SG540 could be fired on full-automatic, single-shot, or in three-round bursts, and it impressed users not only with its quality, but with its accuracy as well. The Legion made some use of the weapon, but it was only intended to be a stop-gap until sufficient FAMAS were available – Manhurin transferred the licence for production to a Portuguese company in 1989.

Although the SG540 was only a temporary expedient, the reputation gained by the gun during its relatively brief period of service meant that the Legion's relationship with SIG rifles would be renewed fairly quickly.

5.56mm FAMAS F1/ G2

The FAMAS is a remarkable-looking weapon. It is of bullpup configuration (that is to say, with the magazine mounted behind the trigger) and can be configured for left-handed shooters by the simple expedient of rotating the extractor and ejection port so that spent cartridges are ejected away from the firer, instead of into his face. The cocking handle is mounted on top of the weapon, shielded by a carrying handle that also contains the FAMAS's sights. The weapon's appearance led to its being nicknamed 'Le Clarion' ('the bugle') by French troops, since, with a little imagination, it can be said to resemble that musical instrument.

The FAMAS F1 is fitted with a folding bipod, making it easier to achieve accuracy with the weapon, although using it leads to a slightly higher firing position than normal, making it more difficult for the user to stay low and out of sight of the enemy. The magazine contains 25 rounds, although to reduce pressure on the magazine spring it is more common for soldiers to load only 22 rounds.

Rifle grenades can be fired from the muzzle, using the 'bullet trap' type of grenade, which does not require special blank cartridges to launch it. Approximately 400,000 of the FAMAS F1 were made before production switched to the G1 and G2 models. The G1 was not produced in quantity, being an interim step to the G2. The G2 is very similar to the F1 model, but has different barrel rifling so that it can use both the M193 and SS109 types of 5.56mm (0.22in) ammunition. The trigger guard is also different, being of the 'full hand' type, which

allows the FAMAS to be fired while wearing heavy gloves. The G2 can also accept standard 30-round M16-type magazines in addition to the old 25-round type. Unlike the F1, the bipod is not fitted as standard to this version.

Despite its appearance, the FAMAS is an excellent weapon, and formed the basis of the next-generation soldier programme being tested by the French Army in 2004. As a result, the FAMAS will be in use for some time to come.

5.56mm Colt M4 carbine

More commonly associated with American units, the M4 carbine is a variant of the famed M16 rifle. It has a shorter barrel, and is fitted with a four-position folding stock. Although not in widespread French use, the GCP teams use the M4, not only because it is more compact than the FAMAS, but also because it is much easier to mount the M203 40mm (1.5in) grenade launcher beneath the barrel, offering the user considerable firepower – in the sort of small-group actions fought by commando forces, this can be of considerable importance.

The M4 can be fitted with an array of sighting devices mounted on a Rail Interface System, another feature which endears it to specialist forces. The M4 has been seen in the hands of GCP legionnaires operating in Bosnia, Rwanda and the Ivory Coast in recent years.

Opposite: A legionnaire stands guard with his FAMAS. The magazine can be seen clearly in this picture. Later models of the weapon have a magazine housing modified to hold the NATO-standard 30-round magazine based upon that used in the American M16 series of rifles.

Sniper Rifles

The Legion has always made considerable use of snipers, with one company of 2 REP specializing in this role. A number of rifles are used, but the three most common are listed below.

FR-F1/FR-F2

The FR-F1 was the standard French sniper rifle for many years, and was an accurate and well-liked bolt-action design with a 10-round magazine. The FR-F1 fired the French 7.5mm (0.29in) cartridge, but by the late 1970s the French Army was looking to use NATO standard rounds. The timing of this decision was dictated by the adoption of the 5.56mm (0.22in) round for the FAMAS, and it seemed appropriate to adopt the 7.62 x 51mm (0.30 x 2in) round for support weapons. As a result, the FR-F2, chambered for this round, entered service in 1984. Both the FR-F1 and FR-F2 have seen considerable service with the Legion. Sniper teams have proved to be extremely effective in peacekeeping operations, particularly in Bosnia. Snipers from the warring parties frequently fired upon civilians during this conflict, and the Legion employed its own snipers to suppress this threat.

7.62mm Accuracy International L96A1

The L96A1 is the standard British Army sniper rifle, firing the 7.62mm (0.30in) round. Designed by the Olympic Gold Medallist Malcolm Cooper, the L96A1 is a highly regarded weapon, and has been added to the Legion's inventory as a complement to the FR-F2. Despite using the same round, the L96 has an effective range 200m (656ft) greater than the FR-F2, and it is for this reason that it has entered Legion use. The weapon has been deployed on recent Legion peacekeeping operations alongside the FR-F2.

.50in Barrett Model 82

The Barrett M82 is one of a formidable range of heavy-calibre sniper rifles now available to the Legion, and is highly accurate up to ranges of 1000m (3280ft) and beyond. It is intended to be used as a long-range interdiction weapon, against both personnel and materiel, with the 12.7mm (0.50in) bullet offering sufficient power to damage vehicles (as well as communications equipment and radar dishes). A high-explosive round can also be used. The M82 is rather heavy, and the recoil forces produced can damage the carefully machined working parts over time. Despite this, the effect that can be obtained by this weapon means that it has proved to be a popular choice with Legion sniping teams.

Right: Legionnaires undertake sniper training in Djibouti during an exercise held in 1995. They are using the standard 7.62mm (0.3in) FR-F2 rifle, an extremely accurate and robust derivative of the earlier FR-F1 which used a French cartridge.

5.56mm SIG SG551/552

The success of the SIG 540 in French service, albeit over a limited period of time, meant that the rifle's replacement on the SIG production line attracted attention from French specialist forces, who are always looking for the best weapons. The SIG SG550 was adopted as the standard Swiss Army rifle in 1984, but the GCPs were more interested in the shorter-barrelled SG551 carbine. As with the SG550, the 551 is an extremely well-made and accurate weapon, and can be fitted with a variety of accessories, including a grenade launcher

beneath the barrel. The SG551 magazine is of innovative design, made from translucent plastic so that the firer can see how many rounds are left in the weapon.

It is also provided with studs and lugs on the side, so that up to three magazines can be joined together, facilitating rapid reloading (20- and 30-round magazines are available). An even shorter model, the SG552 Commando, has now been made, and is very similar to the SG551, although the reduced length means that the firing mechanism has had to be modified to fit. Both are excellent weapons.

Machine Guns

Apart from the terrible Chauchat machine gun used during WWI, the Legion has adopted a range of solid and dependable machine guns, split between French-made weapons and the US Browning classics.

8mm Hotchkiss machine guns

In the 1890s the only viable machine guns were produced by Maxim and Browning, who took great care to patent their products in an attempt to monopolize the market for this type of weapon. The French Hotchkiss company was

Above: French soldiers using a Hotchkiss machine gun during the early part of World War I. The weapon is on an anti-aircraft mounting, rather than the more common tripod. The 25-round magazine strip can be seen protruding from the side of the weapon. The strip was the major source of problems with the weapon, being prone to cause jams when it twisted or became fouled with mud.

8mm Chauchat

Officially known as the *Fusil Mitrailleur Modèle 1915*, the Chauchat ranks as one of the worst weapons ever to have entered service with any army. It was intended as a light machine gun, the need for this type of weapon having been identified at a reasonably early stage in World War I.

It was, however, designed by a committee which sat in late 1914. Inevitably, this design process led to a weapon that was far from perfect. The result was a long, awkward weapon that employed an overly complex firing mechanism. Although this worked, it was difficult to manufacture, and moved inside the gun every time a shot was fired: not surprisingly, this movement, coupled with the recoil, made aiming difficult.

Above: Amidst the carnage of World War I, a legionnaire fires a Chauchat light machine gun from a ruined farmhouse, 1916.

Because of the need for such weapons, contracts for manufacture were handed out to a whole array of engineering firms, many of whom had never built a gun before. The manufacturers often failed to appreciate that certain tolerances were required to ensure that the gun actually worked without fouling, or, worse still, blowing up in the firer's hands because the materials employed were not robust enough.

Many manufacturers took the opportunity to use cheap materials to maximize their profit margins on every gun. Those weapons made in this way were next to useless, quickly breaking after a relatively small number of rounds had been fired. Even when the manufacturers used the right type of materials, the Chauchat was still an awful weapon. It handled badly and jammed at the slightest excuse, as the complicated mechanism did not take kindly to the mud which was one of the major features of the Western Front. In addition to this litany of problems, the decision to fit a

half-moon magazine under the body of the gun made the weapon awkward to carry, while the light bipod was so flimsy that it bent at the slightest provocation.

The Legion was not spared from using this appalling piece of equipment, and many Legionnaires dealt with the gun's problems by simply throwing it away and picking up rifles that had been dropped by dead or injured comrades. The unsuspecting Americans were persuaded to take a version of the gun chambered for their own 7.62mm (0.30in) round, and this proved to be an even worse weapon than the French 8mm (0.31in) version, since the American round was more powerful and caused the poorly made Chauchat to break even more easily.

Unsurprisingly, the Chauchat disappeared from service almost as soon as the war ended. Given that the gun would conceivably have faced even more problems when used in the desert, it is hardly surprising that the Legion was delighted when the last of the Chauchats was withdrawn from use.

one of the first to circumvent this problem when it was approached by an Austrian inventor who described to them a novel method of gas operation to power a machine gun. After convincing themselves that the weapon worked, Hotchkiss quickly purchased and developed the idea.

The first Hotchkiss machine gun was the *Mitrailleuse Hotchkiss Modèle 1897*, which was more of a proof-of-concept than a viable service weapon. It was quickly followed by the *Modèle 1900* and later by the *Modèle 1914*, the latter being the model that was most commonly employed by the French Army during World War I. These models all had air-cooled barrels, but suffered from overheating. The solution was to introduce what was to become a key feature of Hotchkiss weapons in the form of five prominent 'doughnut' collars around the end of the barrel close to the receiver. These rings enlarged the surface area of the barrel at the point where it became hottest and provided greater cooling.

The gun proved popular with a number of armed forces. The French Army made great use of the gun for many years after the war, and some were still in use when the Germans invaded France in 1940. The Foreign Legion was also equipped with the weapon, making considerable use of it to support its

Opposite: A legionnaire on jungle training during the early 1980s is seen carrying an AAT-52 general purpose machine gun. This replaced the Model 1924 in service, and remains in use, although it is being supplanted by the Minimi 5.56mm (0.22in) machine gun.

mobile columns in the desert, with the added firepower being deemed extremely useful given the threat posed by massed charges by North African tribesmen.

However, the Hotchkiss had one notable failing, which was in the way in which ammunition was fed into the gun. Steel strips, each with 24 or 30 rounds, were employed, and this limited the amount of sustained fire that could be produced. Linking strips together was possible, but the linked strips proved prone to damage and fouling, and this often caused feed jams.

7.5mm Fusil Mitrailleur Modèles 1924/29

The French Army was not slow to appreciate the value of the light machine gun for operations during World War I, and made efforts to invest in a suitable design. Sadly, this turned out to be the awful Chauchat, which was manifestly unable to meet the demands placed upon it. After the Armistice, the French Army invested considerable time and energy into developing a much better weapon that would be suitable for deployment in all regions in which the army operated. The result was a weapon based on the Browning Automatic Rifle (BAR), but altered in several ways so that the new 7.5mm (0.29in) cartridge could be employed.

The *Fusil Mitrailleur Modèle 1924* was modern-looking for the time, and employed an overhead box magazine holding 25 rounds. One unusual feature was the use of a dual-trigger system, where squeezing one trigger provided single shots, while using the other gave full-automatic fire. This

system worked, although it was an unusual choice in comparison with the fire selector that was employed on most other weapons, and has not been widely copied.

There were problems with the initial weapon, however, since neither the gun nor the cartridge had been fully developed before it was introduced into service. Alarm spread after a series of internal barrel explosions and other shortcomings were reported by the men equipped with the weapon. The cartridge was redesigned to make it slightly less powerful, while the weapon's parts were made more robust. These modifications were recognized by a change in designation of the gun to *Fusil Mitrailleur Modèle 1924/29*. The alteration solved the problems, and the type became the standard French light machine gun by 1939. When the Germans occupied France, they took over most French stocks of the weapon, although they continued to be employed by French units in the Middle East and North Africa, most notably the Legion. As the weapon was particularly useful, it was returned to production after 1949, remaining in use for many years.

The last were retired once the French Army adopted the AAT-52 General-Purpose Machine Gun. About the only real disadvantage of the FM 1924/29 was the modified cartridge, which gave the weapon a shorter range than many similar machine guns. This did not unduly concern the French Army, however, and they were extensively issued. The Legion made heavy use of the gun, finding it invaluable tool for providing fire support.

Above: During World War II, the Legion made use of the British Bren gun, one of the best weapons of its type ever made. The gun was rechambered from .303-inch (7.7mm) calibre to 7.62mm (0.3in) after the war, and continued in British Army service until the 1990s. This is one of the 7.62mm (0.3in) weapons, differentiated from the .303-inch guns by the Legion by the straighter magazine.

.30in Browning M1919

The Browning M1919 series was derived from the water-cooled M1917 series by the simple expedient of replacing the M1917's barrel with one that was air-cooled. By 1945 the production total was 438,971. Produced mainly for infantry use, the M1919 proved to be an excellent weapon, capable of providing masses of fire while being a robust and reliable weapon. A fabric or metal-link belt was used to feed ammunition to the M1919, which was normally mounted on a tripod. A derivation of the weapon was the M1919A6,

which was produced for use as a light machine gun: it was little more than the MI919A4 model of the gun, fitted with an awkward-looking shoulder stock, a bipod, a carrying handle and a lighter barrel. The result was something of a compromise, since although it provided a useful amount of firepower, it was rather heavy for a light machine gun, and awkward to carry easily.

The Legion came to use some of these weapons simply by virtue of the fact that the Free French forces were supplied with large amounts of American weaponry during World War II, and this remained in

use until indigenous designs could be brought into service. Although not commonly encountered in Legion service, the M1919 was a reliable weapon that did the job asked of it – which was more than could be said for some earlier weapons of this type, particularly the infamous Chauchat.

Opposite: Legionnaires armed with a Browning M1919 machine gun. The M1919 was designed by John Moses Browning, and was an effective weapon that saw front-line service for over 50 years. An air-cooled gun, it could lay down a formidable volume of fire.

.50in Browning M2

The first Browning 12.7mm (0.50in) M2 heavy machine gun was produced in 1921, and the type remains in use today. In fact, it underwent something of a renaissance in service with European armies in the 1980s, when the value of a heavy machine gun was once again appreciated.

From the original Browning M1921 heavy machine gun evolved a whole string of variants based on what was to become known as the M2. On all these variants the gun mechanism remained the same, being very similar to that used on the smaller MI917 machine gun. Where the variants differed from each other was in the type of barrel fitted and the fixtures used for mounting the gun.

One of the most numerous of the M2s has been the M2 HB, the suffix denoting that it is fitted with a Heavy Barrel. The HB version has been employed both for fire support for the infantry and as an anti-aircraft weapon (as well as a fixed or trainable aircraft gun). Given the size and weight of the M2, it is usually mounted on a heavy tripod, or on vehicle mounts.

The Legion uses the M2 in both the mounted and dismounted roles, although the weapon is

Left: A member of 1 RE looks over the vast expanses of Saudi Arabian desert during training prior to the liberation of Kuwait in 1991. He is manning a Browning M2 machine gun mounted atop an armoured vehicle. Although the weapon stems from a design that is over 80 years old, the M2 remains in widespread use simply because it is the best weapon of its type.

Above: Two legionnaires practice firing an LRAC-89 anti-tank rocket system in a training exercise in southern France, 1990. The loader is armed with a FAMAS F1, the standard sidearm of the Legion.

commonly found in later weapons of this type. To assist with aiming, a 12.7mm (0.50in) spotting rifle was mounted on top of the weapon. The rounds from the spotting rifle had the same ballistic properties as the 106mm (4.1in) round, and they enabled the gunner to fire ranging shots. In theory, as soon as one of the 12.7mm (0.50in) rounds hit the target, the Recoilless Rifle could be fired with a high degree of confidence that this round would also hit the target. In practice, this procedure was rather more difficult, not least against targets that were moving.

The bulk of the Recoilless Rifle meant that it could not be employed widely, since it demanded the attention of a two-man crew. In response, designers set about creating lightweight anti-tank weapons firing rockets which could be used by one man, and these were deployed alongside new crew-served anti-tank weapons.

89mm LRAC-89

The French contribution to the earlier generation of anti-tank rockets was the 89mm (3.5in) STRIM, better known in French Army use as the LRAC-89 (an abbreviation of *Lance-Rocket Anti-Char de 89mm*). This was the standard Legion anti-tank weapon for many years, one example of its use being the successes enjoyed by legionnaires using the weapon against rebel armour at Kolwezi in 1978. The LRAC-89 could be operated by just one man, although it was not uncommon to find them being employed by a three-man team made up of an observer to direct fire, the man who would fire the weapon, and a loader. The

more often seen mounted on Legion vehicles.

Anti-Tank Weapons

The Legion has made use of a number of anti-tank weapons since 1945, applying them against enemy strongpoints as well as in their intended role.

106mm Recoilless Rifle

The first anti-tank weapon to see wide use with the Legion was the 106mm (4.1in) Recoilless Rifle. This was a 3m (9.84ft) long weapon mounted on a tripod or on the back of a vehicle, and fired rounds of 106mm (4.1in) ammunition rather than the rocket projectiles more

LRAC-89 remained in Legion service until the late 1980s, but it was gradually replaced by the MILAN anti-tank missile.

115mm MILAN

The MILAN is a crew-served weapon, using a wire-guided missile to ensure greater accuracy. It was built as part of a multi-national collaborative effort, and saw service with the British Army in the Falklands War in 1982 – there were no tanks to engage, so the MILAN was used to destroy enemy bunkers. The bulk of the MILAN means that it is suited for use as a vehicle-mounted weapon, where it can be operated by one man, but for use by dismounted infantry it is not ideal.

137mm Aerospatiale Matra Eryx

To complement the MILAN, the Legion adopted the Aerospatiale Matra Eryx short-range missile. This entered service in 1991. The system can be used at ranges between 50 and 600m (164 to 1968ft), and has proved to be a very precise weapon while on tests. As with the MILAN, the operator of the Eryx has a missile contained in a launch tube which is fitted to a firing unit. The operator launches the missile and controls it via the firing unit, then simply disposes of the empty launch tube. With a weight of under 20kg (44lb), the Eryx is much lighter than a loaded MILAN system, and can be distributed more easily at section level.

Below: Three French soldiers in nuclear, chemical and biological warfare equipment practice with an 89mm (3.5in) LRAC-89 anti-tank weapon. A man-portable rocket, the LRAC-89 was the standard French anti-armour weapon for many years, finally being retired as developments in tank armour rendered its warhead too small to be effective.

84mm AT-4

To provide additional firepower at section level, the Legion has adopted the Swedish AT-4 84mm (3.3in) anti-armour weapon. This weighs less than 10kg (22lb), and is a simple rocket system. The rocket is enclosed in a launch tube that is thrown away after use. All the controls needed to fire the weapon are on the launch tube (as opposed to being a separate item as on the MILAN and Eryx), as are a set of basic flip-up sights. The AT-4 is less accurate than the MILAN or the Eryx, both of which are guided weapons, but it is much lighter and can be carried by a soldier in addition to his normal load of equipment, something that is not the case with the crew-served weapons.

Light Vehicles

The Legion has developed its range of light vehicles not only for transport and reconnaissance, but also to add mobile firepower to its infantry units.

Citroën Méhari Armée

The Citroën *Méhari Armée* was chosen by the French Army as a useful light vehicle for general transport duties. Based on a civilian design, the Méhari was built with an all-steel chassis and a plastic bodyshell. The reason for procuring the vehicle lay in an appreciation of the fact that using cross-country vehicles with four-wheel drive for peacetime transport duties was uneconomical, since it was rare for them to go off road.

Hotchkiss M201

The Free French Forces used American-supplied Jeeps in large numbers during World War II. These were much-admired by the troops, and the need for a light vehicle for post-war service with the French Army prompted the firm of Hotchkiss-Brandt of Paris to obtain a licence for production of the vehicle in France. The first production models of the Hotchkiss M201 were completed in 1953 and by the time production ended in 1969, over 40,000 had been built.

The M201 was almost identical to the wartime Jeep and was employed in nearly as many roles as its American counterpart. It was used as a weapons carrier and fitted with 7.62mm (0.30in) or 12.7mm (0.50in) machine guns, 106mm (4.1in) recoilless rifles (which could also be dismounted from the vehicle for use in the ground role), and the ENTAC anti-tank guided missile. In the anti-tank role, four missiles were carried in the ready-to-launch position in boxes mounted on the vehicle sides, with a further three missiles being carried in reserve.

This model was used for a number of years until ENTAC was replaced by the Euromissile MILAN system. The Legion was particularly keen on using the M201 in the reconnaissance role, and its vehicles were often fitted with communications and surveillance equipment. In common with the rest of the French Army, the Legion replaced its M201s with the larger P4 light vehicle.

Peugeot P4

The Hotchkiss M201 was the standard light vehicle of the French Army from the 1950s , and by the late 1970s the army wished to replace its stock of M201s with a more modern type. A competition was held, in which three manufacturers each provided four vehicles. Peugeot selecting a Mercedes Benz design as the basis of its submission. In 1981 this vehicle, the Peugeot P4, was selected and an order placed for 15,000 vehicles, the first of which entered service in 1982. A versatile light vehicle, some P4s are fitted with twin light machine guns, while others carry MILAN anti-tank teams around the battlefield, each vehicle having one launcher and four missiles.

The Legion has adapted its P4s for use by Regimental Reconnaissance Platoons, and the armament fitted to these vehicles is substantially greater than that applied to P4s of other French units. Weapons fitted include 12.7mm (0.50in) Browning heavy machine guns, AAT-52 General Purpose Machine Guns and MILAN and AT-4 antitank weapons.

Each vehicle has a PR-4G radio set and night-vision equipment. The reconnaissance platoons are divided into command, support and scout patrols. The command patrol has two P4s, one with a 12.7mm (0.50in) machine gun; the support patrol has two MILAN-equipped vehicles, while the three scout patrols each have two P4s. One of these is fitted with a 12.7mm (0.50in) machine gun and an ERYX, while the other has a 7.62mm (0.30in) machine gun and an AT-4. In combination, the P4s of the Regimental Reconnaissance Platoons possess formidable firepower, offering Legion formations a versatile force that can be used to provide mobile fire support as well as carrying out its basic reconnaissance function.

Above: Taken in January 1954, this photograph shows an American M151 Willlys Jeep being used to take Marc Jacquet, the French Minister for Associated States, on a visit round Dien Bien Phu. The Jeep served as a model for the almost identical Hotchkiss M201, which was used until the 1980s.

Armoured Cars and Light Tanks

As a light rapid-response force, the Legion has not used the heavy armour of more regular armoured formations. It has, however, relied on various light tanks and armoured vehicles to provide its reconnaissance units with a more

powerful defensive capability, including the ability to take on enemy armour should their be no other option.

M8 Armoured Car

The most important American armoured car of the World War II, over 11,000 M8s were built by 1945.

The main armament of a 37mm (1.45in) gun was accommodated in an open turret, while a 12.7mm (0.5-inch) machine gun was often carried on a ring mounting above the turret itself. French forces were issued with the vehicle in lieu of any home-built armoured cars, and made considerable use of them in

177

Above: Vietnamese troops march in front of a 1 REC M24 Chaffee during an operation against Viet Minh guerrillas. The American-made Chaffee proved ideal for the conflict in Indo-China, its 75mm (3in) gun being an excellent support weapon, while its array of machine guns (including a 12.7mm (0.50in) seen mounted on the turret) were employed against massed enemy infantry assaults.

Indo-China. While the 37mm (1.45in) gun had been inadequate for dealing with tanks, it was an ideal weapon for providing fire support for ground troops. The M8s were eventually replaced by Panhard EBR armoured cars.

M24 Chaffee

The Chaffee was developed from the recognition that the 37mm (1.45in) gun fitted to the M3 and M5 series of light tanks was inadequate for dealing with all but the most lightly-armoured opposition. The M5 was unable to accommodate a larger gun, which led to the initiation of design studies for a tank that could mount a 75mm (3in) gun. The M24 Chaffee was the result. The

M24 had a crew of five, larger than might have been expected for a light tank, and with a secondary armament of three machine guns in addition to the main gun, had more firepower than had been traditional for such a vehicle.

The Chaffee saw relatively limited service in the last eight months of World War II, and remained in American service until the 1950s. The French obtained Chaffees after the war, and they saw much use in Indo-China. At Dien Bien Phu, 10 M24s fired more than 15,000 rounds of 75mm (3in) ammunition providing fire support in just one infantry action.

Panhard EBR

The Panhard EBR armoured reconnaissance vehicle was used by the Legion for many years. It had its origins in a 1937 design for an armoured car with outstanding cross-country mobility. A prototype of this vehicle was completed in 1939, but the outbreak of World War II prevented any further development. At the end of the war, the French Army was in desperate need of new equipment. A great deal of this was provided by the United States and Great Britain, but it was all of World War II vintage. The French Army issued a requirement for a brand new armoured car, and after studying several proposals, awarded contracts for prototypes to the Panhard and Levassor concern and another to Hotchkiss. The Panhard design, an eight-wheel-drive vehicle that drew its inspiration from the 1937 vehicle, was chosen and entered service in 1950. Production continued for 10 years, and ended after 1200 vehicles had been produced.

The EBR had a crew of four men, comprising the commander and gunner, and two drivers. The

Above: A column of Panhard VAB armoured vehicles pause outside the Bosnian enclave of Zepa during the Yugoslavian civil war. The confused mandate given to peacekeeping troops meant that it proved almost impossible to protect refugees until NATO took over responsibility with far more robust rules of engagement.

Above: A mixed column of French and American troops pass by two abandoned cars during the Iraqi retreat from Kuwait. The VAB armoured personnel carriers proved ideal for the fast paced-pursuit.

drivers sat in positions at the front and rear of the vehicle, a useful feature for the reconnaissance role. The driver in the front could take the EBR towards the enemy so that reconnaissance could be conducted, and when the time came to leave, the driver at the rear of the vehicle would take over – in effect, the EBR did not reverse,

of the vehicle were fitted with steel rims. This feature enhanced cross-country mobility by improving traction over soft ground. The steel-rimmed wheels were raised off the ground when travelling on roads, turning the vehicle into a 4x4. The EBR was fitted with potent armament for an armoured car, in the form of an oscillating turret fitted with a 90mm (3.5in) gun and a co-axial 7.5mm (0.29in) machine gun. The main gun was capable of dealing with most enemy tanks of the 1950s, and 43 rounds of ammunition were carried onboard.

Despite having a gun more commonly found on tanks, the purpose of the EBR was not to seek out and engage enemy tanks or support advancing infantry. Crews were strongly discouraged from gaining any thoughts about trying to become 'tank aces' should they find themselves engaged in a major battle against an opponent equipped with armour.

Initially, thoughts of using these vehicles in a major European war were not of great concern to the Legion, since they were based in Algeria. The mobility conferred by the EBRs was of great use in patrolling the vast expanses of desert that faced the French in their attempts to quell the uprising by the FLN.

After the Legion left Algeria for the final time, the EBRs remained in use, their role now being primarily that of armoured reconnaissance in a major conflict. However, given the Legion's function as a rapid deployment force, it was little surprise that the EBRs were used overseas, either as part of a self-contained deployment by *1er*

Régiment Etranger de Cavalerie (1st Legion Cavalry Regiment; 1 REC), or to provide support for other Legion regiments. The EBRs were finally retired from French service in the 1980s, although they had already been replaced in Legion service by the Panhard AML series of armoured cars.

Panhard AML

The Panhard AML was chosen by the French Army as a replacement for British-built Ferret Scout cars, which had been used in North Africa during the 1950s. Recognizing the value of a wheeled armoured car, the French took the opportunity to write a specification that called for a 4x4 vehicle that had a range of armament options beyond the machine gun carried by the Ferret.

The result was the Panhard AML, which entered production in 1960. The vehicle has a three-man crew, and in the AML-90 variant is armed with a 90mm (3.5in) gun and two 7.62mm (0.30in) machine guns. The second most common version is the AML-60, armed with a breech-loaded 60mm (2.4in) mortar. The Legion made extensive use of both vehicles, finding the 60mm (2.4in) mortar particularly useful for indirect fire support. There were a number of versions of the 60mm (2.4in) mortar vehicle. The HE 60-7 was fitted with two 7.62mm (0.30in) machine guns alongside the mortar; the HE 60-12 replaced the two machine guns with a 12.7mm (0.50in) heavy machine gun, and the HE 60-20 had a single 20mm (0.79in) cannon.

The AML enjoyed considerable success in Legion service, proving

since it was always going in the direction of the driver controlling the vehicle. The EBR's eight wheels were unusual in that the pair of centre wheels on each side

AMX-10RC

By the early 1970s, the standard French heavy armoured car, the Panhard EBR 90, had been in service for 20 years. Although the EBRs had life in them yet, the decision was taken to develop a new vehicle. In the late 1960s, the French Army issued a requirement for a new armoured car that would have a more powerful gun and a sophisticated fire-control system, good cross-country performance, and be fully amphibious. The result was the AMX-10RC, the first of which began trials in the mid 1970s, with service entry occurring in 1979. While the AMX-10RC was an excellent vehicle, it proved to be extremely expensive (costing more than some main battle tanks), and this prompted the French Army to reduce the numbers it intended to buy.

The vehicle is fully amphibious, with two waterjets at the rear of the hull acting as the propulsion system. These provide a maximum water speed of 7.2km/h (4.5mph). Perhaps the most notable feature of this versatile vehicle is its heavy main armament, in the form of a 105mm (4in) gun which is able to tackle most targets that the AMX-10RC is likely to encounter, with the exception of modern main battle tanks. The 105mm (4in) gun has 40 rounds of ammunition provided for it, and a 7.62mm (0.30in) machine gun is mounted alongside it (this has 4000 rounds). Two electrically operated smoke dischargers are mounted on each side of the turret and fire forwards, providing a useful screen should the vehicle need to withdraw in a hurry.

The fire-control system was the most sophisticated of its type installed in any armoured car, and is arguably still the best fitted to any vehicle of this type. It includes a laser rangefinder, a fire-control computer and a low-light TV system with a screen for both the commander and driver. The fire-control system enables stationary and moving targets to be engaged as effectively in darkness as in daylight.

Although the French Army order was reduced,

Above: A column of AMX-10RCs move across desert terrain during the 1991 Gulf War. They were employed in their traditional reconnaissance role as well as being used as the spearhead of the rapid French advance into Iraq.

this did not affect the re-equipment of 1 REC with the AMX-10RC, which has seen extensive use, notably in peacekeeping operations in the former Yugoslavia. A valuable piece of equipment, there is currently no sign of a suitable replacement entering service, and the Legion is likely to use the AMX-10RC for some years yet.

to be a reliable and popular vehicle with 1 REC. The Legion began to dispose of its AMLs in the late 1970s, replacing them with the larger and notably more expensive AMX-10RC.

Aircraft

The Legion has relied upon transport aircraft not only for tactical mobility and logistical tasks, but also for para-dropping operations in places such as Indo-China, Zaire and Algeria.

C-47 Dakota

The Douglas DC-3 was designed as a commercial airliner in the 1930s, but was pressed into service in large numbers during World War II. Known as the C-47 Skytrain to the US Army Air Forces, and the Dakota to the British, the aircraft saw service in all theatres of war. Amongst its many tasks was para-dropping, most notably during the invasion of France in June 1944, and the air assault at Arnhem a few months later.

The Dakota also provided valuable resupply to British troops fighting in Burma (1942–45). At the end of the war, the British and Americans provided the French with a number of Dakotas to give them an air transport fleet.

These saw use in Indo-China, and were employed for the first operational parachute drop made by the Legion in 1949. The Dakota remained in service with the French for some years, but was superseded by the Nord Noratlas and the C-119 Flying Boxcar. The latter aircraft was loaned to the French Air Force by the Americans, and returned after the war in Indo-China ended.

Above: A Panhard EBR armoured car (right) stands in the shadow of a Bregeut Provence transport aircraft. The EBR's twin pairs of metal-rimmed central wheels, designed to improve cross-country mobility, can be seen clearly here, in their raised position.

Nord 2501 Noratlas

At the end of World War II, the French Air Force was equipped with a mixture of aircraft from Britain, the United States and even captured German machines.

While most of these were perfectly adequate for the tasks they were called to perform, the French set about rebuilding their aircraft industry. The main transport types available were the Douglas C-47 Skytrain and captured Junkers Ju-52s. Both were excellent aircraft, but not ideal for military transport tasks because of the limitations imposed by their having a side door – loading vehicles was particularly difficult, as they had to be manhandled through a relatively narrow gap.

As a result, a specification was issued in 1947 for an aircraft that could be loaded through 'clamshell' doors at the rear, allowing vehicles to be driven straight on to the aircraft. The Nord 2501 Noratlas was selected, being notable for a twin-boom layout to meet the vehicle-loading requirement. Over 400 of these robust aircraft were built, and they saw widespread service. They were used to transport Legion paratroops in Indo-China, in Algeria during the war of independence, and also in Chad in 1984 over 30 years after the aircraft entered service.

The Noratlas was also used by Portugal, Greece and Israel, as well as by a number of African countries. A popular aircraft, the Noratlas was overshadowed by more famous American-made contemporaries, but was the workhorse for Legion para-dropping for over 30 years.

C-130 Hercules

The most famous and most widely used transport aircraft of the modern era, the C-130 entered service with the US Air Force in 1956. The French Air Force bought a total of 14 a decade later, and they are employed mainly in the strategic transport role.

They are familiar to the men of the Legion, since they have been used to ferry legionnaires around the world. The men of 2 REP have an even deeper acquaintance with the type, however, since it is used alongside the Transall C.160 for parachute training. Four C-130s were used by 2 REP to parachute into Kolwezi in 1978, although these aircraft were provided by the Zairian Air Force rather than the French.

Transall C.160

The Transall C.160 was one of the first collaborative ventures between European aircraft manufacturers, and was designed to supplement and ultimately replace the Noratlas in French and German service. The first production aircraft appeared in 1967, and when manufacturing ended in 1972, some 169 aircraft had been built.

Production reopened in the late 1970s as the French sought another 25 aircraft to replace the last of the venerable Noratlas. Able to carry 88 paratroops, the C.160 has been the main aircraft used by the Legion for parachute training and operations in the last three decades, including the rescue mission by 2 REP at Kolwezi in 1978.

Above: An AML armoured car unloads from the back of a Transall C.160 during manoeuvres in the Ivory Coast in 1981. 1 REC practiced this type of airfield assault, in which armour was unloaded directly from transport aircraft onto the objective, with the infantry force required usually joining the fray by parachute.

Campaigns of the Legion

DATE	THEATRE	UNITS INVOLVED
1831–35	**Algeria**	**Old Legion**
	Campaign against the Emir of Mascara, Abd-el-Kader	
1832	Battle of Maison-Carree	
1832	Battle of Sidi-Chabal	
1835	Battle of Mouley-Ishmael	
1835	Battle of Macta	
		(Legion casualties: 844)
1835–39	**Spain**	**Old Legion**
	Campaign against the Carlist army	
1836	Battle of Tirapegui	
1836	Battle of Zubiri	
1837	Battle of Huesca	
	Heavy defeat for the Legion	
1837	Battle of Barbasto	
		(Legion casualties: 1103)
1836–49	**Algeria**	**New Legion**
1837	Battle of Djebel Dreuth	
1837	Assault on Contantine	
1839	Battle of Djidelli	
1839	Battle of Col de Tizi	
1840, 12 May–14 Jun	Battles at Col de Mouzaia	
1843	Sidi-bel-Abbés becomes headquarters of 1 RE	**1 RE**
1844	Battle of M'Chounech	**2 RE**
1849, May–Sep	Operations in the oasis of Zaatcha	
1854–55	**Crimea**	**1 RE, 2 RE**
	France, Britain and Turkey against Russia	
1854	Battle of Alma	**1 RE, 2 RE**
1854	Battle of Inkerman	**1 RE**
1854-55	Siege of Sebastopol, 1 RE's commander, Colonel Vienot is killed in the action	
		(Legion casualties: 444)
1857	**Algeria**	
	The Legion wins the Battle of Ischeriden	**2 RE**
1859	**Italy**	
1859, 4 Jun	Battle of Magenta	**1 RE, 2 RE**
1859, 24 Jun	Battle of Solferino	**2 RE**
		(Legion casualties: 143)
1863–67	**Mexico**	**Foreign Legion Regiment**
1863, 30 Apr	Battle of Camerone	
1863, 12 Sep	Battle of Cotastla	
1865, 16 Jan–8 Feb	Siege of Oajacca	
1866	Battle of Santa Isabel	
		(Legion casualties: 468)

DATE	THEATRE	UNITS INVOLVED
1870–71	**Franco-Prussian War**	**Foreign Legion Regiment**
1870, 10 Oct	Action before Orleans	
1870, 9 Nov	Battle of Coulmiers	
1871, 19 Jan	Battle of Montchevis	
1871, Apr–May	Siege of Neuilly	
		(Legion casualties: 930)
1870–82	**Algeria**	**1 RE**
1870	Abd-el-Aziz leads Berber revolt against the French	
1882	Battle of Chotti Tigri	
	Berbers are defeated.	
		(Legion casualties: 655)
1883–85	**Indochina**	**1 RE**
1883	Capture of Son-Tay	
1884	Capture of Bac-Ninh	
1884, 3 Jan–3 Mar	Siege of Tukyen-Quang	
1885	Capture of Lang-Son	
		(Legion casualties: 370)
1892–94	**Dahomey and the Sudan**	**1 RE**
1892, 19 Sep	Battle of Dogba	
1892, 4 Oct	Battle of Porguessa	
1892, 3 Nov	Battle of Ouakon	
1892, 17 Nov	Capture of Abomey	
1892, 13 Oct	Battle of Ackpa	
		(Legion casualties: 39)
1895–1904	**Madagascar**	**1 RE**
1895, 9 Jun	Battle of Maratanano	
1895, 22 Aug	Capture of Andriba	
1896, 22 Nov	Battle of Mahatsara	
1896, 20 Dec	Capture of Maroakoha	
1898	Battle of Soaserena	
		(Legion casualties: 260)
1903–34	**North Africa**	**1 RE, 2 RE**
1903	Battle of El Moungar	
1907	France establishes protectorate in Morocco	
1908	Battle of Menabha	
1911	Battle of Alouana	
1914	Revolt of the Riffs in Morocco led by Abd-el-Krim	
1918	Battle of Gaouz	
1922	Battle of Scourra	**3 RE**
1926	Revolt of the Riffs in Morocco is crushed	
1933	Battle of Djebel Sagho	**2 RE**
		(Legion casualties: 2100)

DATE	THEATRE	UNITS INVOLVED
1914–18	**France**	
1914, *Dec*	Argonne	**1 RE**
1915, *May*	Battle of Artois	**1 RE**
1916, *Jul*	Battle of the Somme	**RMLE**
1917, *Aug*	Battle of Cumieres	**RMLE**
1918, *Apr*	Battle of Hangard Wood	**RMLE**
1915–18	**The Near East**	**Regiment**
1915, *Jun*	Gallipoli	**de Marche**
1915, *Dec*	Serbia	**Algerie (RMA)**
1916, *Nov*	Battle of Monastir	

(Legion dead in World War I: 4931)

1925	**Syria**	
1925, *Jul*	Battle of Kafer	**4 REI**
1925, *Sep*	Battle of Messifre	**4 REI, 1 REC**
1925, *Nov*	Battle of Rachaya	**1 REC**
1939–45	**World War II**	
1940	Battle for France	**11 REI, 12 REI 21, 22 & 23 RMVE**
1940	Operations at Narvik	**13 DBLE**
1941	Syria, Free French fight Vichy forces	**6 REI, 13 DBLE**
1942	Defence of Bir Hakeim	**13 DBLE**
1943	Tunisia	**1 REIM**
1944	Campaign in Italy, invasion of France	**13 DBLE, 1 REC, RMLE**
1945	Campaign in Germany	**RMLE, 1 REC, 13 DBLE**

(Legion casualties in campaign: 9017)

1947–54	**Indochina**	
1948	Battle at Phu-Tong-Hoa	**3 REI**
1949	Action at Ninh-Phuoc	**2 REI**
1950	Action around Dong-Khe	**3 REI, 1 BEP**
1951	Battle at An-Hoa	**13 DBLE**
1954	Defence of Dien Bien Phu	**1 & 2 BEP, 2 & 3 REI, 13 DBLE, 5 REI**

(Legion casualties in campaign: 10,483)

1954–62	**Algeria**	**1 & 2 RE, 2, 3,**
1957	Battle of Algiers	**4, & 5 REI,**
1961	Rebellion against de Gaulle, 1 REP is disbanded	**13 DBLE, 1 & 2 REC, 1 & 2**
1962	Algerian war ends	**BEP, 1 REP**

(Legion casualties in campaign: 1855)

1956	**Egypt** Anglo-French landings at Suez	**1 REP, 2 REC**
1967	**Algeria** Last Legion unit leaves the country	**1 REC**
1969–70	**Chad** Intervention to restore order	**2 REP**

(Legion dead: 8)

DATE	THEATRE	UNITS INVOLVED
1976	**Djibouti** Rescue of schoolchildren from terrorists	**2 REP, 13 DBLE**
1978	**Zaire** Legion rescues European settlers in Kolwezi	**2 REP**

(Legion casualties: 5)

1978–79	**Chad** Second French intervention	**2 REI, 2 REC**

(Legion casualties: 1)

1982–83	**Lebanon** Legion forms part of multinational peacekeeping force in Beirut	**2 REP, 2 REI, 1 RE, 1 REC**

(Legion casualties: 5)

1983–84	**Chad** Third French intervention	**1 REC, 2 REP**
1990	**Gabon** Deployment to safeguard French citizens	**2 REP, 2 REI**
1991	**Gulf War** French forces participate in UN-led action against the Iraqi invasion of Kuwait	**13 DBLE**
1992–present	**Balkans** Legion units part of European and UN peacekeeping forces in Bosnia and Kosovo	
1994	**Rwanda** Legion forces provide humanitarian aid & security	**2 REP**

Bibliography

Bergot, Erwan. **The French Foreign Legion.**
London: Wingate, 1975.

Cadiou, Yves L & Tibor Szecsko. **French Foreign Legion: 1940 to the Present.** London: Arms & Armour Press, 1986.

Debay, Yves. **French Foreign Legion Operations, 1990–2000.** Marlborough: The Crowood Press, 2000.

Geraghty, Tony. **March or Die: France and the Foreign Legion.** London: Harper Collins, 2001.

MacDonald, Peter. **The Making of a Legionnaire.**
London: Sidgwick & Jackson, 1991.

McLeave, Hugh. **The Damned Die Hard: The Story of the French Foreign Legion.** Farnborough: Saxon House, 1974.

Murray, Simon. **Legionnaire: The Real Life Story of an Englishman in the French Foreign Legion.**
London: Pan Books, 2001.

O'Balance, Edgar. **The Story of the French Foreign Legion.** London: Faber & Faber, 1961.

Paris, Bill. **The Making of a Legionnaire: My Life in the French Foreign Legion.**
London: Weidenfeld & Nicholson, 2004.

Porch, Douglas. **The French Foreign Legion.**
London: Macmillan, 1991.

Price, G Ward. **In Morocco with the Legion.**
London: Jarrolds, 1937.

Simpson, Howard. **French Foreign Legion Paratroopers: From Vietnam to Bosnia.**
London: Brassey's, 1999.

Stone, David. **Dien Bien Phu.** London: Brassey's, 2004.

Wellard, James. **The French Foreign Legion.**
London: Andre Deutsch, 1974.

Windrow, Martin. **The Last Valley: Dien Bien Phu and the French Defeat in Vietnam.** London: Orion, 2004.

Windrow, Martin & Kevin Lyles. **French Foreign Legion Paratroops.** Oxford: Osprey Publishing, 1985.

Windrow, Martin & Mike Chappell. **French Foreign Legion Infantry and Cavalry Since 1945.**
Oxford: Osprey Publishing, 1996.

Windrow, Martin & Mike Chappell. **The French Indo-China War 1946–1952.** Oxford: Osprey Publishing, 1998.

Windrow, Martin & Mike Chappell. **The Algerian War, 1954–1962.** Oxford: Osprey Publishing, 1997.

Windrow, Martin & Mike Chappell. **French Foreign Legion, 1914–1945.** Oxford: Osprey Publishing, 1999.

Young, John Robert. **The French Foreign Legion: The Inside Story of the World-Famous Fighting Force.**
London: Thames & Hudson, 1984.

Index

Page numbers in *italics* refer to illustrations.

PICTURE CREDITS

Every effort has been made to trace the copyright holders for all photographs and illustrations used in this book. However, if you believe that you are the copyright holder and have not been approached, then please contact Amber Books.

Cody Images: 7, 31 (Peter MacDonald), 34, 66, 68, 74, 75, 76, 77, 78, 79, 80, 82 (ECPA), 83 (ECPA), 84–85, 86 (ECPA), 88, 95, 96, 111, 122, 124 (Peter MacDonald), 132, 142 (Peter MacDonald), 150, 151, 152, 154-5, 158–9, 160, 161, 166 (U.S. National Archives), 167, 170, 171, 174 (Yves Debas), 175, 178, 180-1, 184, 185;

Corbis: 18-19, 35, 42, 56, 58, 69, 70, 72, 91, 92, 97, 99, 101, 104, 105, 108, 109, 113, 126, 127, 128, 129, 130, 131, 134, 136, 146, 156, 172–3, 179;

Katz Pictures: 98 (Gamma), 102 (F. Spooner), 107 (Gamma), 110 (Gamma), 114 (Gamma), 115 (F. Spooner), 116 (F. Spooner), 117 (©Zed Nelson), 120 (©Zed Nelson), 121 (F. Spooner), 137 (F. Spooner), 140 (F. Spooner), 141 (Gamma), 144 (©Zed Nelson), 147 (Gamma), 148 (©Duclos Merillon), 163 (F. Spooner), 164-5 (Gamma), 168 (B.Gysembergh/Gamma), 182–3;

Képi Blanc: 11, 14–15, 16, 17, 20, 21, 24–25, 48, 64–65;

Mary Evans Picture Library: 39, 44–45, 53, 54;

Military Picture Library International: 123, 139, 145;

Popperfoto: 177;

Roger Viollet: 71;

Topham Picturepoint: 9, 13, 22, 23, 27, 27, 28, 32–33, 37, 47, 57, 59, 60, 62, 90.

All maps by Patrick Mulrey.